Four Insights for Finding Fulfillment

成就的祕訣：金剛經

Other Works by Venerable Master Hsing Yun:
Life
For All Living Beings
Being Good
Humanistic Buddhism: A Blueprint for Life
Chan Heart, Chan Art
Humble Table, Wise Fare

Sutra Commentaries:
The Universal Gate:
A Commentary on Avalokitesvara's Universal Gate Sutra
The Rabbit's Horn:
A Commentary on the Platform Sutra
The Great Realizations:
A Commentary on the Eight Realizations
of a Bodhisattva Sutra
Sutra of the Medicine Buddha

FOUR INSIGHTS

for

Finding
Fulfillment

Venerable Master Hsing Yun

Translated by Robert Smitheram

Buddha's Light Publishing, Los Angeles

© 2012 Buddha's Light Publishing
First edition

By Venerable Master Hsing Yun
Translated by Robert Smitheram
Book design by John Gill and Wan Kah Ong

Published by Buddha's Light Publishing
3456 S. Glenmark Drive
Hacienda Heights, CA 91745, U.S.A.
Tel: (626) 923-5144
Fax: (626) 923-5145
E-mail: itc@blia.org
Website: www.blpusa.com

Printed in Taiwan.

Library of Congress Cataloging-in-Publication Data

Xingyun, da shi.
    [Cheng jiu de mi jue. English]
    Four insights for finding fulfillment : a practical guide to the Buddha's Diamond Sutra /
Venerable Master Hsing Yun ; translated by Robert Smitheram.
        p. cm.
    Contains English translation of Kumarajiva's Chinese translation of Diamond Sutra—
publisher's e-mail.
    ISBN 978-1-932293-54-8
    1. Tripitaka. Sutrapitaka. Prajñaparamita. Vajracchedika—Commentaries. I. Kumarajiva,
d. 412? II. Tripitaka. Sutrapitaka. Prajñaparamita. Vajracchedika. English. III. Title. IV. Title:
Practical guide to the Buddha's Diamond Sutra. V. Title: 4 insights for finding fulfillment.

    BQ1997.X45913 2011
    294.3'823--dc23

                                                                        2011028646

Contents

Acknowledgments

Like all of Buddha's Light Publishing's endeavors, this project benefited from the contributions of many people. We would like to thank Venerable Tzu Jung, the Chief Executive of the Fo Guang Shan International Translation Center (FGSITC), Venerble Hui Chi, Abbot of Hsi Lai Temple, and Venerable Yi Chao, Director of FGSITC for their support and leadership.

Robert H. Smitheram provided the translation; John Gill, Susan Tidwell, and Louvenia Ortega edited the texts; and Wan Kah Ong and Amanda Ling proofread the manuscript and prepared it for publication.

Our appreciation goes to everyone who supported this project from conception to completion.

Editorial Note

Four Insights for Finding Fulfillment quotes liberally from a variety of Buddhist texts and other sources. In particular, Master Hsing Yun visits and revisits many passages from the *Diamond Sutra* as he draws out its key insights.

◇ A full English translation of the *Diamond Sutra* has been provided as an appendix to the text. To assist the reader in finding the relevant passages in the sutra and gaining a sense of context, a diamond icon, as seen to the left, has been placed next to sizable quotations from the sutra to indicate which of the sutra's thirty-two chapters the quote is referencing.

Preface

Success in the Human World

In the history of Chinese Buddhism there are three Buddhist sutras which are regarded as "core texts." These are the *Heart Sutra* and the *Diamond Sutra* as spoken by the Buddha, and the *Platform Sutra* as spoken by Huineng, the sixth Chinese patriarch of the Chan School of Buddhism.

Kumarajiva, one of the most well-known translators of Buddhist sutras into Chinese, translated the *Heart Sutra* into Chinese in the fifth century during the Later Qin dynasty. By the seventh century, another translation by Xuanzang made during the Tang dynasty became the one with the widest currency among the Chinese public. The translation of the *Diamond Sutra* used in this book is Kumarajiva's translation, and the one most widely circulated, though Xuanzang did retranslate the *Diamond Sutra* as well. Two of China's great translators expended large amounts of time and effort to translate the *Heart Sutra* and the *Diamond Sutra*, clearly demonstrating just how extraordinary and important these two Buddhist sutras are.

The mere mention of the *Diamond Sutra* calls to mind Buddhism, and likewise any mention of Buddhism brings to mind the presence of the *Diamond Sutra*. Today most Buddhists who recite the *Diamond Sutra* do so to ask for protection against ill fortune and pray for good fortune and long life. When someone passes away, their family and friends as well as Buddhist monastics will recite the *Diamond Sutra* to help the person find a better rebirth. Everyone from great monastics to the public at large read and recite this sutra. The language of the *Diamond Sutra* is beautifully refined and possesses an excellent rhythm, such that even if one does not understand its meaning, reciting it or hearing it read can bring peace and joy to one's heart.

I wrote my *Introduction to the Diamond Sutra*[1] in 1997, a text of nearly three hundred thousand Chinese characters, in which I arranged and explicated the meaning of this sutra. Today, a dozen or so years later, I've endeavored to write the present volume as a way of sharing a practical method for achieving success and fulfillment contained within the *Diamond Sutra*.

The Sanskrit title of the *Diamond Sutra* is *Vajracchedika Prajnaparamita Sutra*. But what do words like *vajra, prajna,* and *paramita* mean? And how are we to understand and practice the *Diamond Sutra*?

The *Diamond Sutra* relates a series of questions and answers that take place between the Buddha and his disciple Subhuti, regarded as the Buddha's foremost disciple in understanding emptiness. Their dialog expounds on the empty nature of *prajna,* and asserts that "all phenomena lack an inherent self" and "all phenomena are transient." Once we thoroughly understand emptiness, this understanding will benefit us and allow us to be successful in whatever we do, in both worldly and spiritual pursuits.

Four Insights for Finding Fulfillment shares my belief in the

---

1. Selections were published in 2001 as *Describing the Indescribable*.

ability to apply the Dharma in the human world. The Dharma must be put into practice. We cannot separate ourselves from our experiences, nor can we separate ourselves from the larger community of human beings. We can use the elements of our daily lives to succeed in our practice and deepen our faith. It is as Huineng said:

> Daily, constantly practicing to benefit others,
> Attaining Buddhahood
>   does not come from giving money.
> *Bodhi* is found within the mind
> Why bother looking
>   for the extraordinary outside?

It is not enough to read the sutras, we must also practice them. Learning Buddhism is meant to bring fulfillment right here, in the human world; after all, what aspects of our daily lives cannot be applied to spiritual practice? "*Prajna*" is the "secret ingredient" to this kind of success.

Besides quoting from the *Diamond Sutra* and the other great wisdom texts of Buddhism, I will also supply supporting material from Buddhism's treasury of *gongans*. Called *koans* in Japanese, they are the stories of generations of great practitioners of the Chan School. Their wisdom is like a lamp casting light on a room that has been darkened for thousands of years. It is my hope that, even amidst this hectic modern life, that everyone can gain some understanding, for once one gains realizations they, too, become a shining source of light.

One can say that the *Diamond Sutra* has four main teachings: to give without notions, to liberate with no notion of self, to live without abiding, and to cultivate without attainment. The principles articulated by the Buddha more than two thousand years ago can not only be applied to each of us individually and to the Buddhist monastic order as a whole, but they can also be applied to any organization or enterprise. As a monastic disciple of the Buddha, teaching the Dharma for the benefit of living beings has been both a joy and a responsibility, and I think about the *Diamond Sutra* from time to time and try to practice its four main teachings such that I "believe it, receive it, and practice it" just as mentioned at the close of the sutra.

It is my hope that everyone will find fulfillment and grasp the secret to success from the *Diamond Sutra* and become great successes in this world!

Hsing Yun
September, 2010

I

Parami

True Success

"Success," as it is generally understood, is nothing more than personal success in the present lifetime, things like fame, wealth, and power. In the teachings of Mahayana Buddhism, "success" means benefiting living beings, having successful cultivation, and becoming a Buddha or bodhisattva.

Quite a number of people believe that for Buddhist monastics to develop from ordinary people into sages they must cut themselves off from their family and loved ones and hide away in some remote mountain hermitage. Likewise, there is a saying in Buddhism that "All things are empty," though this concept of "emptiness" is often misunderstood to mean that we should not want or pursue anything. This misapprehension recasts the Buddhist teaching on "emptiness" into nothing but meaningless talk about metaphysical ideas. But, according to Buddhism, success comes as the fruition of karmic causes and conditions. These instances of karmic fruition are also called *paramitas*.

Parami is an ancient Sanskirt word which means "to cross over," in that one crosses from the shore of suffering over to the other shore of *nirvana*, while "*ta*" is an auxiliary particle that indicates completion. When the Buddhist sutras were translated from Sanskrit to Chinese, the choice was made to transliterate the term *paramita*, rather than translating its meaning, and most English translations follow in suit. This was done in order to preserve the concept as close to the time of the Buddha's transmission of the Dharma and not to limit it by a particular translated term.

If we want to cross over affliction, trouble, and the cycle of birth and death, and transform suffering into happiness, partiality into universality, and affliction into enlightenment, we must rely upon the six *paramitas*. Also known as the "six perfections," the six *paramitas* are six methods that enable us to cross over and transcend. The six *paramitas* are giving, morality, patience, diligence, meditative concentration, and *prajna*. Each of the *paramitas* will be explained more fully later.

The four main teachings of the *Diamond Sutra* are to give without notions, to liberate with no notion of self, to live without abiding, and to cultivate without attainment; this way of practicing the Dharma allows us to cross from this shore to the other shore and to fulfill our *paramitas*. To put it more simply, one should use a spirit that transcends the world to do the work of the world.

Human life can be divided into four levels:

1. Physical life
2. Community life
3. Transcendent life
4. Unending life

"Physical life" refers to the physical body as given to us by our parents. This human body is hard to come by, so we should take good care of it. "Community life" means fulfilling one's role within the larger life of the group. "Transcendent life" means altruistically contributing what you can for the sake of others, the larger community, and for all living beings. "Unending life" refers to what Buddhism calls the "life of wisdom." Someone who lives this way is not worried about whether he lives or dies, having transcended the suffering of life and the fear of death. This is eternal life where one no longer wanders through the cycle of birth and death.

Every human life has boundless potential. It is up to the mind of each individual to fulfill the value and success of life.

Reconsidering Value

In her later years, my mother was a patient at Whittier Hospital in Los Angeles, U.S.A. On May 31, 1996, I received news in Taipei that my mother's illness had taken a turn for the worse, and I immediately boarded a plane for Los Angeles. During the flight I kept reflecting on the past. In my mind I could see my mother's tender, smiling face as if it were before my very eyes. My heart filled with all manner of emotions, and I silently recited the name of Amitabha Buddha as a blessing for my mother.

Upon arriving at Los Angeles International Airport, I raced over to the hospital, but my mother had already passed on. All I could do was go over to Rose Hills Memorial Park to pay my last respects.

The nursing staff that had been looking after her told me that she was kind and frugal, and was plain and simple in her daily needs. She rarely bothered others and was always thinking of other people. My mother did not even want them to tell me about her worsening condition, to spare me any alarm or worry. My mother always took everything upon herself, and kept her feelings of care and loving concern inside. Twenty minutes before she died, she still left instructions with Venerable Tzu Chuang, the abbess of Hsi Lai Temple who was attending at her side:

> Thank you for reciting the name of Amitabha Buddha on my behalf. I am leaving now, so, please, under no circumstances are you to let my son know, thus sparing him any distress. He should busy himself with the problems of all sentient beings and not be troubled on my account alone.

In the face of disciples and family members who had hurried to Los Angeles from various places, I decided to follow my mother's final instructions by not disturbing the outside world and keeping everything simple. In accordance with her wishes, no formal condolences, no funerary contributions of money and no gifts or flowers were accepted. I then dictated the following obituary notice to solemnly inform all those concerned:

> My mother, Mrs. Liu Yuying, peacefully passed away at 4:20 A.M. on the 30 of May, 1996, at Whittier Hospital in Los Angeles, U.S.A, amid the sounds of chanting "Amitofo." She was ninety-five years old. Many of her children and grandchildren as well as my disciples were by her side. Her body was then transferred to Rose Hills that same day.

Four days later, my mother was cremated at Rose Hills. Amid the sounds of those assembled there chanting sutras and reciting Amitabha Buddha's name, I gently pressed the green switch to activate the cremation process. At that time I composed the following poem in my mind:

> Between this mundane world and the Pure Land,
> There remains the unchanging bond
>   between mother and son;
> For whether here on earth or there in heaven,
> She remains forever my dear mother.
> With a burst of fire,
> A puff of wind,
> And a flash of light,
> I bid eternal farewell to my mother.

My mother was twenty-five when she gave birth to my body. Since then seventy years had slipped away, and my mother has passed on. And so, with a push of a button, the body of my mother was cremated. Our physical bodies are like houses that we live in only for a short time. Time passes and the house becomes leaky and in need of repair. This temporary residence of ours will surely decay, and there will come a time when we will be unable to live in it anymore.

Some twenty years earlier, my mother once came to stay for a while at Fo Guang Shan, and on one occasion during a grand assembly of lay disciples, I asked whether or not she was willing to meet with them and say a few words. She agreed, but I was worried that my mother would be intimidated by stage fright. But to my surprise, she faced the assembled audience of more than twenty thousand and said with a calm assurance, "Fo Guang Shan is indeed the Western Pure Land of Ultimate Bliss; a heaven on earth. We should rely upon the venerable master to be our guide in the hope that everyone will achieve enlightenment here at Fo Guang Shan. Everyone has been so kind to me, but this old woman has nothing to give to you in return. I can only offer my son as a gift to everyone."

Her words were met by thunderous applause from the audience. My mother was illiterate and had never read any sacred literature, nor ever prepared herself to speak in front of others. But she had experienced the chaos of the late Qing dynasty, the Revolution of 1911, the establishment of the Republic of China, the armed occupations of the warlords, the Sino-Japanese War, the stand-off between the Nationalist Party and the Chinese Communist Party, and the Great Cultural Revolution, as well as the changes over time in relations between Taiwan and Mainland China.

The turmoil of the times had kept her constantly on the move; she lived through nearly one hundred years of epoch-making change. In her life, she practiced the Dharma, but she was too busy to let the question of whether or not she had a firm background in Buddhism bother her. She had already transcended the scriptural understanding with all its careful wording to bring fulfillment to her own life.

And yet, through the power of a vow, we have the power to return again to this human world.

Humanistic Buddhism

As Buddhists we acknowledge that the Dharma exists in the world, but what exactly is the Dharma as taught by the Buddha?

The word *Buddha* means "enlightened one," for he is one who has enlightened himself, enlightens others, and has completed his mission of enlightening others. A Buddha is one who transcends the ignorance of sentient beings. The quality of his enlightenment is unlike that of the *sravaka* or *pratyekabuddha*, who pursue enlightenment for themselves alone. A Buddha has realized a state of enlightenment that even a bodhisattva has yet to fully attain.

The founder of Buddhism was originally named Siddhartha, though he is also called Sakyamuni Buddha, the World-honored One, the Tathagata, and so on. He was born on the eighth day of the fourth month of the lunar calendar in Lumbini Garden within the Indian state of Kapilavastu. His father, King Suddhodana, was head of the Sakya clan. His mother, Queen Maya, died seven days after his birth.

Sakyamuni Buddha was raised into adulthood by his maternal aunt, Lady Mahaprajapati. As a prince, Siddhartha was a handsome and intelligent young man, who was skilled in both the civil and military arts. From boyhood, he was much beloved by the common people. His father put all his effort into training him to become a wise ruler. When he was seventeen, Siddhartha married the beautiful Yasodhara, and the following year she bore him a son, Prince Rahula.

However, despite his life in the palace with all its comfort and contentment, and the warm love and affection of his family, Siddhartha felt a deep void in his heart. He was seeking something more from life and needed a truer understanding of human existence. So at the age of twenty-nine, he bid farewell to his family, gave up all his pleasures and comforts, and left the palace to pursue his spiritual quest. At age thirty-five, after six years of austere practice, he sat underneath the bodhi tree, and attained enlightenment while looking up at a bright star, and said, "Marvelous, marvelous! All sentient beings have the Tathagata's wisdom and virtue, but they fail to realize it because they cling to deluded thoughts and attachments."

The now enlightened Buddha shared his realization with others, setting the wheel of Dharma turning, and established the monastic order. He then taught the Dharma for the liberation of living beings for forty-nine years, and entered *nirvana* while lying between two sala trees outside the city of Kusinara in the year 483 BCE.

The Buddha was born in this human world, grew up and attained enlightenment in this human world; he passed into *nirvana* in this human world, as well. Buddhism has always been concerned with this human world. The Buddhist sutras which circulate today are a record of the Buddha's teachings to liberate living beings, gathered and organized by his disciples after the Buddha's final *nirvana*. From the time of the Buddha, the Buddhist teachings are meant to fundamentally address the issues of how we as human beings are to conduct ourselves, how we are to act and think throughout the course of our lives, as well as how we can gain liberation. The Dharma quite naturally serves as a guide to how to live our daily lives. As Buddhism enters the modern era, we as Buddhists must take an active role in the world and be diligent.

There are some people who think the Dharma serves as an escape, that one may "retreat into Buddhist practice," as if Buddhism is some sort of pessimistic escape or resignation that does not demand that we accomplish anything. The *Ekottara Agama* states:

> All the Buddhas and World-honored Ones come from the human world; their realization is not something attained in the heavenly realms.

Huineng, the Sixth Patriarch of the Chan School, also said in the *Platform Sutra:*

> The Dharma is within the world, apart from this
> world there is no awakening. Seeking *bodhi* apart
> from the world is like looking for a rabbit's horn.

If we seek enlightenment by rejecting the world, in doing so we throw away our potential. This creates a sense of withdrawal and escape in the mind, and then nothing whatsoever will succeed.

Buddhism is not a religion that belongs only to monastics, nor is it a body of philosophical texts to be studied by scholars. Buddhism should be something that benefits all people. Buddhism is not an abstract theory; it is a religion that brings happiness and well-being into the world. To learn Buddhism is to learn how to be happy, carefree, liberated, and attain meditative bliss and Dharma joy. Joy and happiness are the most precious things in life, and living a happy, blessed, and carefree life is what Humanistic Buddhism promotes. Humanistic Buddhism is the practical application of the Buddhist spirit in the world.

One day, the Buddha and his disciples entered the city of Sravasti to gather alms, and it so happened that they encountered someone who bore a grudge against the Buddha. This person started to malign, slander, and shout in a loud voice as the Buddha walked along the street.

Seeing how the Buddha was being insulted in public, one of his disciples said to the Buddha angrily, "The people here lack any speck of goodness and do not know how to respect the Triple Gem. Lord Buddha, it would be better if we left this place and went to a city with kind-hearted people!"

The Buddha replied, "Suppose we do move to another place but the people there still do not believe in the Dharma, what would you do then?"

The disciple said, "We should move to yet another place!"

"When will we ever stop moving if we do so because of external conditions? This is not the way to ultimately solve the problem! We can resolve the root of the problem this way: If we are treated with scorn, we must remain unperturbed and bring an end to slander through patience. We must not stop guarding our speech and training our minds until we are no longer treated with scorn."

The Buddha continued, "An enlightened person remains calm and patient like the earth. We should not allow our mission to be shaken by either praise or blame. By contemplating the absence of an independent self, we will observe how all phenomena are false fabrications. Then the illusory distinctions of self and others, as well the so-called good and bad of the world, will become nothing more than froth upon the water that suddenly appears, and just as suddenly disappears. Can anything remain constant and unchanging?"

Buddhism such as this is what allows people to experience well-being and success. It is a religion for people, and one that is concerned with the development of people. In Buddhism there is a teaching called the "three Dharma seals," which are three qualities that certify something as an authentic teaching. They are all conditioned phenomena are impermanent, all phenomena are without an independent self, and *nirvana* is perfect tranquility. By viewing the world through the teaching on impermanence, one can come to understand that all conditioned phenomena are impermanent. Determination and diligence allows us to see that "all phenomena are without an independent self." In Buddhism there is a saying that "there is nothing to attain," and it is because of this understanding that all the wonders of existence can arise out of true emptiness. The last of the three Dharma seals, "*nirvana* is perfect tranquility" asserts that our potential for success is unlimited.

Wholesome Wealth

There are many people in this world who believe that one of the standards for measuring success is making a lot of money. In terms of material wealth, Buddhist monastics live a plain and simple life: they live with three robes, a bowl, and few small items, such as sutras and a Buddha statue. There is even a saying in Chinese that, "A monastic's rucksack weighs only two and a half pounds." That being said, even a skilled housewife cannot prepare a meal without rice, and a poor couple will suffer hundreds of sorrows. A lay Buddhist must have some monetary wealth, or else he will be unable to care for his parents and support his family. Buddhist practice and acts of charity also require a certain amount of money to support them, let alone the riches required to engage in various social development programs. Therefore, Humanistic Buddhism does not disdain money, for wealth that is acquired through pure and wholesome means can serve as supporting resources.

However, we must also understand that worldly success arises from a combination of causes and conditions. Consider the example of a single individual. The process that takes this person from birth as a crying baby to maturity as an adult is supported by many causes and conditions, such as the safeguarding by parents, instruction of teachers and elders, as well as the various trades and professions that supply clothing, food, housing, transportation and so on. We go to school, find our place in society, start a family, and begin our careers; and we all hope we will be successful in these. But success is not building castles in the sky, nor is it possible to achieve it without hard work. Having the right conditions in place to support us is to our advantage, but even then depending upon others too much cannot lead to success either.

People are often greedy. If they have even a bit of money, they think of depositing it in the bank where it will accumulate interest. But in that case, such money cannot be used to launch new enterprises. We bring no money with us when we are born, and take none of it with us when we die, and during our lives it is always taken away by fire, flood, thieves, corrupt officials, and wayward children.[1] We can only appreciate the value of money if we do not feel attached to it, but rather allow our wealth to circulate and accomplish good things. There is a Buddhist saying that captures this sentiment well:

> What comes from all directions
> Supports undertakings in all directions;
> The generosity of thousands of people
> Creates connections for thousands of people.

In this way worldly money can serve both worldly causes, as well as those that transcend this world.

There are some people who have a fixed view that spiritual practice does not need money and cannot involve money, and expect spiritual seekers to live in poverty. But poverty cannot guarantee a higher level of practice. These attitudes come from a fixed sense of self which is attached to appearing impoverished, that it is the only way to be a practitioner. This is a question of reality. If you have nothing, how then can you give something? To liberate living beings and practice giving, we need the qualities of physical strength, practical talent, ability, and commitment. Why must monetary wealth be singled out for disdain and rejection? To

---

1. These are the "five causes of loss": five things mentioned in the Buddhist sutras that can destroy our wealth. *Ed.*

varying levels, lacking mental or material resources will limit our ability to give and liberate others.

The question that is truly worthy of our concern is how to best utilize the pure, wholesome, and noble wealth that is donated to benefit living beings. We should not fall into the view that only poverty can show that one is well cultivated. For a modernized Buddhism, Buddhists should engage in enterprise so long as such activities are beneficial to the economy of the country and the lives of its people. This then is the true meaning of the Buddhists teachings on "non-abiding" and "non-self."

Oneness and Coexistence

There is a story recounted in the *Samyukta Agama* about two monastics who argue about who is better at chanting. One day the Buddha's great disciple Mahakasyapa reported to the Buddha, "Lord Buddha, there are two monks who are both unyielding in nature; one is Ananda's disciple Nantu and the other is Maudgalyayana's disciple Abifu. The two of them argue with each other from time to time over who is the best at chanting, and tomorrow they are going to decide once and for all who can chant the most sutras and teach the Dharma the best!"

The Buddha sent someone to summon Nantu and Abifu. He then asked them, "Have you heard my teaching on how to determine the winner and the loser when two people are arguing with one another?"

"We have never heard of such a teaching concerning winning or losing."

"The real winner is someone who puts a stop to the confusion caused by greed, anger, and ignorance; diligently practices the threefold training of morality, meditative concentration, and wisdom; and can destroy the thieves of the six sense organs. One who can truly contemplate how the five aggregates of form, feeling, perceptions, mental formation, and consciousness are as insubstantial as a plantain trunk; and can make the Noble Eightfold Path their guide can realize the bliss and tranquility of great *nirvana*. You may be able to recite hundreds of thousands of verses from memory, but if you do not understand their meaning, then how does that benefit your liberation?"

The Buddha wants us to cultivate right concentration, part of the Noble Eightfold Path, and stay away from any conflict between ourselves and others. The *Diamond Sutra* emphasizes how one should not abide in anything. In terms of human commercial enterprises, one must not become attached to a single fixed market. Do not cling to old markets and old industries, but have the courage instead to open up alternative avenues, seek out alternative markets, and set up new creative teams. By implementing strategies like "value reassessment," "collective creation," and "systematic leadership," one can develop brand new enterprises and live a life as vast as endless space.

Value Reassessment

In the *Diamond Sutra*, the Buddha instructs living beings to not cling to the notion of self, the notion of others, the notion of sentient beings, or the notion of longevity, nor to allow the discriminating mind to hinder our practice. If organizations and commercial enterprises are able to align themselves closely with human nature, be attentive to the needs of the larger community, and offer more varied opportunities, then they can create new value.

In the past, hearing Buddhist teachings required a visit to a temple, but since such temples were located in remote locations with poor transportation, people often hesitated to go. Even the infrastructure of the temples failed to meet the needs of those who came to hear the teachings. Having done their best to visit once or twice, some beginning Buddhists would give up on their good intention of listening to the Dharma.

The *Lotus Sutra* states:

> In whatever land where this sutra is received and upheld, read and recited, explained and copied, and cultivated and practiced as taught; whether in a place where a volume of scripture is kept, or in a grove, or in a forest, or under a tree, or in a monastery, or in a layman's house, or in a temple hall, or in a mountain valley, or upon an open plain; in all of these places one should erect a memorial stupa and make offerings. Why is that? One must know that these places are temples.

The *Vimalakirti Sutra* also states:

> The upright mind is a temple, the profound mind is a temple, the mind aspiring to *bodhi* is a temple, generosity is a temple, the three kinds of supernatural knowledge[2] are a temple, the knowledge of all phenomena within a single thought is a temple.

---

2. The three kinds of supernatural knowledge are knowledge of past, present, and future lives, heavenly eyes, and the power of ending all defilement. *Ed.*

That is to say, everywhere in the world can be a place for us to learn the Dharma and attain enlightenment. In order to spread the Dharma throughout the world, it should go into homes, schools, factories, farms, workplaces, and military bases. By upholding the principles of harmonizing the traditional and the modern, by sharing ownership between monastics and laypeople, by equally emphasizing both practice and understanding, and by integrating literature and art with Buddhism, we will continue to promote Humanistic Buddhism.

Fo Guang Shan and its branch temples all include facilities like auditoriums, conference rooms, classrooms, lounge areas, reception areas, and libraries, along with the gradual addition of the Fo Guang Yuan art galleries, Water Drop teahouses, and so on. Such an approach allows devotees to come to the temple not only to worship the Buddha, but also to receive the Dharma instruction that is offered in auditoriums, conference rooms, and classrooms. In this way Fo Guang Shan endeavors to combine the worldly with that which transcends the world, and integrate society with the mountain monastery, so that monastics and laypeople can practice anytime and anywhere.

With its transcendent spirit and worldly practicality, Buddhism liberates living beings by bestowing upon them the Buddha's wisdom and compassion. The enterprises of the world with their profit motive must also adapt to changes in external conditions from time to time, so that they can provide the products and services that are aligned with the people's demands in a planned, organized, and efficient manner. That too is using a spirit that transcends the world to do the work of the world.

Collective Creation

Organizations and enterprises must create new value, but this is impossible to accomplish by relying solely on one individual to take charge of everything and make all the decisions. What is needed is for everyone to pull together their creative ideas and the will for collective success.

In its early days, Fo Guang Shan had absolutely nothing. We had neither modern equipment nor today's popular management theory, but what we did have was group planning and effort, and the tacit understanding we all shared about collective creation. In 1967, the construction of the temple began, and I brought along the first generation of my disciples—Hsin Ping, Hsin Ting, Tzu Chuang, Tzu Hui, and Tzu Jung—and together we began to toil and work. We cleared away each tree and moved every rock. We drafted the general layout for the temple's structure in the Lichee Garden, and came up with our teaching guidelines in the old Huiming Hall.

At each stage in going from nothing to something, there were perhaps personal differences over understanding, conceptualization, and judgment, but once an issue affected the general direction of Fo Guang Shan, or what was needed to bring success to Buddhism, everyone promptly came together. There was never any conflict sparked by personal or selfish motives, for we shared a common determination to overcome any difficulties and help each other work towards the same goal. This was the spirit behind the founding of Fo Guang Shan.

"Collective creation" does not mean many people supporting the dictatorship of one individual; rather, it means that each individual within the collective participates equally, so we can broadly solicit views and opinions from all corners. From Fo Guang Shan's founding to the present day, nearly every single issue has been decided democratically. At all of our meetings at every level of the organization, everyone has an equal opportunity to speak and exercise their right to vote, regardless of their degree of seniority or the duties they undertake. At the meetings I chair personally, anybody who is so inclined is free to sit in and listen at any time. Not only does this style reduce many of the barriers to getting things done, it also ensures that members of Fo Guang Shan who attend these meetings can learn the art of communication. Everyone has an opportunity to grow from such experiences.

When I think of Fo Guang Shan's initial building phase, images of how all of us worked together from morning to night, shouldering loads of bricks, sand, rock, and cement with sweat streaming down our backs flash in my mind. After the hired workers had finished their day's work and gone home, Fo Guang Shan's disciples would continue working. In addition, there are no words to describe the assistance we received from all of the laypeople who wished to support the Dharma. This is why I often say, "the success of Fo Guang Shan belongs to everyone." Fo Guang Shan is not for any individual. Rather, it belongs to its more than thirteen hundred monastic disciples, the millions of lay followers around the world, its many benefactors, as well as people from all walks of life. Fo Guang Shan was not something that was completed in a day or a certain period of time; it succeeded, bit by bit, through the continuous effort due to oneness and coexistence.

Systematic Leadership

Even during the Buddha's time the monastic community had a well-developed organizational system. The Buddha set up the *posadha* system, in which monastics met regularly to reflect upon their religious lives and confess their faults, and the *karman* system for conducting meetings and adopting resolutions. In these systems we can see a set of legal procedures that are even more complete in their details than those of many modern countries. The Buddha's management style reflects a deep understanding of human nature and his system of rules and regulations are skillfully adaptive. The Buddha's monastic community could be ranked among the best of the many successful enterprises we have today.

Never in my life have I worried about my future, and I have not set my mind on any particular achievement. Things just fell into place naturally. The year I turned fifty-eight, I relinquished my position as abbot of Fo Guang Shan, but even then I was merely stepping down in accordance with the system. I then left Fo Guang Shan and went directly to Beihai Temple. I wanted to let my successor get on with the job, which is why I did not want to linger at Fo Guang Shan. In Buddhism there is a saying that one should "rely on the Dharma rather than an individual"; organizations and enterprises, likewise, need clearly defined and implementable system as they pursue success.

The Buddha's Light International Association, a Buddhist organization founded to encourage the participation of lay Buddhists, has a membership now in the millions, while the entire Fo Guang Shan organization operates harmoniously. We have furthered the work of spreading the Dharma to all parts of the world, and each of our successes has been achieved by operating within our system.

In this way the Dharma has been able to break through the barriers of race, language, and culture, and we have been able to use Buddhist chanting, calligraphy, writing, publishing, and visual and performing arts to spread Humanistic Buddhism to every corner of the world.

The success of Fo Guang Buddhists can be seen as an example of "cultivation without attainment": in Fo Guang Shan, we have a policy that glory belongs to the Buddha, and the success belongs to the community. In this instance these achievements "belong" in the sense that each person contributes their cultivation without expecting to gain anything in return. In this way, Fo Guang Buddhists are one with all living beings, and can coexist together in harmony.

Building One Brick at a Time

In Chinese there is an old saying: "When the eggs are not ready to hatch, do not crack the shell; when the rice is not fully cooked, do not lift the lid." Trying to break open the eggs when they are not ready to hatch will bring an untimely death to these small creatures, and trying to lift the lid of the pot before the rice is fully cooked will make it hard for the rice to be cooked tender.

There is no free lunch in this world. If you want to get something you must give something. I would suggest that, when a person is young, he or she should fear neither hardship, nor being at a disadvantage. One should harden oneself with real experience with no expectation of compensation. One should increase one's own knowledge and experience, no matter if that be through reading books, starting a major undertaking, or engaging in some sort of work. Do not be eager for success: success that comes too

easily can lead to pride and disdain for others, and with such ir-
resolute aspirations, one will quickly fail and be laid low. A lofty
tower is built from the ground up: no real success in this world
is achieved all at once. Success does not happen by mere chance,
nor is it a product of instant results. Rather, it is solidly built one
brick at a time. Great minds often develop gradually. Likewise,
there is a saying in Taiwan that goes: "a big rooster takes its time
crowing."

Quick success is not really all that good. Take trees for example: those that mature in a year are only good for firewood, while
those that mature in three to five years can be made into tables
and chairs. Only trees that take decades and decades to mature can
be made into pillars and beams. That is why we should "cultivate
without attainment," and free ourselves of that win or lose mentality that leads to hasty work. We must gradually cultivate and
refine ourselves, and wait until the conditions are right. As it is
said, the journey of a thousand miles begins with the first step; so
never get ahead of yourself nor delude yourself with the idea that
chanting Amitabha Buddha's name for two days will give you a
diamond-like mind capable of overcoming evil.

After Hongren, the Fifth Patriarch of the Chan School, gave the
monastic robe and alms bowl to Huineng, signifying that he was
now the Sixth Patriarch, he escorted Huineng to a riverbank and
said to him:

> Henceforth, you shall spread the Dharma far and
> wide. You should depart now and quickly travel
> south. Do not start teaching too quickly because it
> is difficult to spread the Dharma.

The Fifth Patriarch was telling Huineng not to be too eager to spread the Dharma publicly. It is important to wait for the right opportunity. This was why Huineng lived in seclusion among a band of hunters, eating some vegetables that he added to their pot of meat, as he bided his time. A favorable opportunity is when all the conditions are right. Any matter can easily succeed, if it happens at just the right moment when the causes and conditions are in place.

The Ten Directions and Three Time Periods

People often ask me, "The Fo Guang Shan monastic order is large and its activities are on an immense scale, how do you manage it all? How do you keep everyone focused, harmonious, and without contention?"

I always like to reply by sharing an old Buddhist expression: "Pervade across the ten directions and extend down through the three time periods."[3]

The expression "Pervade across the ten directions and extend down through the three times periods" describes our own intrinsic Buddha nature. The size of everything in the world is limited, the only things large enough to "pervade across the ten directions" are *prajna*, our intrinsic nature, and the Dharmakaya. Such things are so large that nothing is outside them and so small that nothing more can be contained within; for they pervade everyplace and exist everywhere. In terms of time, although our physical bodies are

3. 橫遍十方，豎窮三際: The ten directions are the four cardinal directions, the four intermediate directions, plus above and below, and the three time periods are the past, present, and future. There is a suggestion in the Chinese expression that space exists on a horizontal plane and that time exists on a vertical plane, with the two together encompassing everything. *Ed.*

born and die and our lives come to an end, our intrinsic Buddha wisdom can transcend the temporal limitations of past, present, and future. It neither arises nor ceases and does not come or go, which is why it "extends down through the three time periods."

The year I stepped down as abbot of Fo Guang Shan my successor, Venerable Hsin Ping, would come and ask me the same question whenever any major event was about to take place at the monastery. He would ask, "How should we handle it this year?"

I would always answer, "Look to what was done before."

Referencing earlier precedents means striving for consistency with the monastery's guiding principles, yet as times change, all things should also undergo some reform and innovation. This is why I said to look to what was done before, not to follow what was done before.

To build people's faith in the Dharma I have gone from riding a bicycle down to the village in my early years to taking automobiles. Because of this modernized society, instead of walking, I can now fly to and fro through the sky. I deeply appreciate how these modern forms of transportation offer many conveniences for teaching the Dharma. However, an appropriate respect for tradition can allow people to see the true meaning of Buddhism. For example, beginning in 1988 and continuing every other year afterwards, Fo Guang Shan has an alms procession, in which monastics collect donations with their bowls as in the time of the Buddha. Not only does this activity serve to bring the light of the Buddha's compassion to every corner of Taiwan and give Buddhists an opportunity to make offerings and generate merit, it is a good experience for the monastics as well. In 1988 I launched a series of events across Taiwan entitled "Returning to the Buddha's Time," featuring ceremonies, performances, and a Dharma talk. The events used modern audio-visual multimedia to enable the audience of tens of thousands to travel back in time and return to the sacred site of Vulture Peak where the Buddha was teaching twenty-five hundred years ago and share in the Dharma joy of Buddhist chanting.

The policy of referring to past precedents is a manifestation of "extending down through the three time periods." Whenever some improvement is introduced, it goes through a process of discussion and coordination and then later becomes widely known to everyone. Meetings are an indispensable part of this process. There are times when students ask to attend our meetings, and I do not refuse them.

In the past I served on the monastery staff, and while taking care of guests I developed a keen awareness as to how all things are connected. Each moment can be considered as a point that leads to some other point, together these points make a line, and by observing many of these lines, one comes to an understanding of the whole. By seeing some individual matter as part of the whole, then one can tweak its temporal and spatial qualities in just the right way so that nothing will be left out.

Buddha nature permeates everywhere, "pervading across the ten directions and extending down through the three time periods." Because of this, in terms of our essence, both the Buddha and I possess the same Buddha nature. Therefore, I need not submit to force, nor become beguiled by wealth and honor. I am one with all living beings. Sometimes I may sit upon a high throne and expound the sublime truths of the Buddha, while at other times I can toil and work for the benefit of living beings and contribute through my sacrifice. I can be great or be small, I can come first or come last, I can do with or do without, I can handle happiness or suffering, I can expand or contract, and I can bear being full or being hungry. I was not born with the ability to do everything, but I am always willing to try.

It is because of the maxim "pervade across the ten directions and extend down through the three time periods" that we must throw open the universal gate. There can be no racial barriers or special treatment. We must be able to lead people from all walks of life, regardless of their religious and social backgrounds, into sharing equally in the benefits of the Dharma. This will enable all living beings from different regions of the world and different stations in life to benefit from the Dharma's various positive connections, and bestow them upon society.

Buddhist Success: Paramita

As mentioned previously, *paramita* is a Sanskrit word that means "success," "crossing from this shore to the other shore," and "the perfect tranquility of *nirvana*."

We know that we must go from this shore of delusion and cross to the other shore of enlightenment, but can we do this just by thinking about it from time to time?

The *Diamond Sutra* says we should "Give rise to a mind that does not abide in anything." In this instance, "abide" means to be attached to something, particularly attached to an independent self. When we become too focused on this sense of an independent self we become attached to the perceived value of this "self," and thus cling to certain ideas and never let them go. When we worry too much about the gains and losses of this "self" our feelings become deluded by love, hate, sadness, and happiness. Having a mind that does not abide in anything calls upon us to live in the world according to the selflessness of *prajna*, for this is the only way to reach the state of *nirvana. Nirvana* is:

- Complete tranquility
- The highest bliss
- Everlasting happiness
- Complete merit and wisdom
- Total freedom from desire
- The ultimate state of liberation
- True reality

Success in Buddhism is transcending this shore with its affliction, delusion, and suffering, and crossing to the other shore of purity and tranquility, where no afflictions appear and all suffering has ended. The specific practice to accomplish this is a group of virtues called the "six *paramitas*" or "six perfections." The six *paramitas* are

1. Giving (*dana-paramita*)
    Giving is to take what one has or knows and give it to others. Besides the giving of wealth and property, this also includes giving the Dharma and confidence or fearlessness to others. The *paramita* of giving can help to eliminate the defilement of greed.

2. Morality (*sila-paramita*)
    The basis of Buddhist morality is the five precepts, but it is not enough to think that the five precepts are just about not doing this or not doing that. The five

precepts should be viewed in positive terms, for that is the path to happiness. For example, one should go beyond the first precept "not to kill" and in addition actively protect life. One can go beyond "not stealing" and practice giving. One can go beyond "not committing sexual misconduct" and be respectful. One can go beyond "not lying" and give praise. Going beyond not killing to protect life leads to a long life; going beyond not stealing to practice giving brings riches; going beyond not committing sexual misconduct to being respectful leads to a pleasant family life; and going beyond not lying to giving praise means that one will have a good reputation.

3. Patience (*ksanti-paramita*)
   In Buddhism there are three kinds of patience: the patience for life, the patience for phenomena, and the patience for non-arising phenomena.[4] A bodhisattva is one who patiently endures all the humiliations of life, as well as cold, heat, hunger, thirst, and so on. The *paramita* of patience can help to eliminate the defilement of anger.

4. Diligence (*virya-paramita*)
   The *paramita* of diligence includes physical diligence and mental diligence. Mental diligence means earnestly practicing wholesome teachings while taking care to eliminate the roots of unwholesomeness. The

---

4. This type of patience comes from the realization that, on a supramundane level, phenomena do not truly arise or cease, and all things are simply as they are. *Ed.*

paramita of diligence is the antidote for laziness and idleness.

5. Meditative Concentration (*dhyana-paramita*)
    The *paramita* of meditative concentration comes from making one's mind free of distractions such that it does not become confused or deluded by worldly matters. The *paramita* of meditative concentration can remove the defilement of doubt.

6. Prajna (*prajna-paramita*)
    The *paramita* of *prajna* is the most important of the *paramitas*, and the forerunner of the other five. By using *prajna* wisdom one can eradicate the defilement of ignorance.

I loved playing basketball when I was young, so I often draw my analogies from basketball: be it spiritual cultivation, academic study, or interacting with others, they're all like playing basketball. For example, when trying to get along with others, you should not go off to fight your own battles, for it is important to remember team spirit. One should wait for the right time to act, just as when one has possession of the ball, one must wait for any opportunity to make a shot. And if you break the rules, you must admit your fault, just as in raising one's hand in a game.

When playing basketball, one must have the spirit of the six *paramitas*: you must pass the ball to your teammates to help them to score points on a basket (giving), you need to play by the rules of the court (morality), you must show restraint to avoid being bumped by others during the heat of a match (patience), you must practice your skills if you want to score (diligence), and, in addition to fundamentals, you must develop basketball strategy in order to win (*prajna*).

Why is *prajna* considered the foremost *paramita*? The *Treatise on the Perfection of Great Wisdom* says, "the other five perfections are blind without *prajna* to guide them." It is impossible to reach the ultimate goal by relying only upon the other five *paramitas* and attempting to do without *prajna*. This is why *prajna* is described as the foundation of the six *paramitas* and is also the foundation of the Dharma.

The *Lotus Sutra* states, "The turmoil of the three realms is like a burning house." The three realms of Buddhist cosmology (the desire realm, the form realm, and the formless realm) are like a burning house. But if we make our minds nice and cool, then the blaze of suffering that presses upon us will disappear. Only by cultivating *prajna* without the expectation of gain can we succeed with the six *paramitas*.

Once the Chan master Caoshan Huixia said to his attendant, "An enlightened person will be unperturbed by heat, no matter how hot it gets inside or outside."

Huixia's attendant agreed. Huixia then asked, "If it were extremely hot now, where would you go to escape it?"

The attendant answered, "I would seek refuge in a burning-hot cauldron."

Huixia was puzzled. He asked further, "Nothing is hotter than a cauldron. Why would you seek refuge in such blazing heat?"

Pointing at his heart, the attendant answered, "The great mass of suffering cannot reach me here."

The *Diamond Sutra* reveals to us the secret of success: to have a mind that does not abide in anything. This is *prajna*. The mind itself is all of wondrous existence, while abiding in nothing is true emptiness; and there cannot be wondrous existence without true emptiness. The *prajna* of the Buddha can make one understand the mind and body with crystal clarity, like the moon reflected in water, transporting one from this shore of delusion and attachment to the other shore that is permanent, blissful, pure, and has an inherent self. Practitioners are able to turn a world of blazing heat into a realm that is refreshingly cool, and transform defilement and affliction into the Pure Land. Such people find no situation in which they are not content.

II

Prajna

Life's Secret Ingredient

Once, as an assembly of his disciples gathered atop Vulture Peak, the Buddha held a flower in his hand. Everyone was silent, and only the venerable Mahakasyapa responded with a smile.

The Buddha then spoke: "I have the treasury of the true Dharma eye, the wondrous mind of *nirvana*, the true reality without form. It is a profound teaching that is not set down in written words, but is a separate transmission beyond the teachings. This I entrust to Mahakasyapa."

The Buddha stepped in front of the Bahu-putraka Stupa, shared his seat with Mahakasyapa, and spread out his outer robe, enshrouding the two. The Buddha then said to Mahakasyapa, "I entrust the treasury of the true Dharma eye to you. Protect and maintain it for future generations."

ॐ ॐ

The above story is very famous in Buddhism. It is called the *gongan* of "holding forth a flower and responding with a smile," and is recorded in the *Combined Sources from the Five Lamps*, which traces the lineage of the Chan School of Buddhism back to the Buddha's transmission of the Dharma to Mahakasyapa at that very assembly on Vulture Peak. In front of all the people there, the Buddha and Mahakasyapa shared what is called "mind-to-mind transmission." Rather than being an explanation mediated through language, such a transmission goes directly to the intrinsic mind, thus breaking the cycle of contradiction and misunderstanding created by language.

Later on, Bodhidharma, the twenty-eighth Indian patriarch of the Chan School, came east to China to teach the Dharma. Bodhidharma taught a style of wall-gazing meditation that could make the mind peaceful by pointing directly to the way things are, which is *prajna* itself. Five generations of disciples later this teaching was passed to Hongren and then onto Huineng, the sixth Chinese patriarch, under whom the Southern School of Chan witnessed a tremendous surge in growth, fulfilling Bodhidharma's prophecy:

> A single flower will open with five petals,
> Bearing fruit when the time is right.

What Is Prajna?

From the past to the present day, those wishing to understand *prajna* mostly do so through a careful reading and understanding of the Buddhist sutras. Dharma teachers in the past would explain every word and comment on each sentence as they went from sutra to sutra. A teaching on one Buddhist sutra would often take several months, sometimes lasting even a year and a half. It is recorded that when the great Tiantai master Zhizhe was teaching the *Lotus*

Sutra, his explication of the first character in the title, *miao* (妙), "wondrous," went on for ninety days. This event would later be remembered by history as "three months on the character *miao*."

In the time after Sixth Patriarch Huineng, the Chan School was divided into the Southern School, which taught sudden enlightenment, and the Northern School, which taught gradual enlightenment. The Southern School used the *Diamond Sutra* in their mind-to-mind transmission, while the Northern School used the *Lankavatara Sutra*. Huineng's first connection with the Dharma was forged when, in his hometown of Lingnan, he heard someone reciting the *Diamond Sutra*. Later on he went to Huangmei and heard Fifth Patriarch Hongren give a teaching on the *Diamond Sutra*, and upon reaching the passage "give rise to a mind that does not abide in anything," Huineng suddenly awakened.

Upon receiving the Fifth Patriarch's mind-to-mind transmission of the Dharma, Huineng became the Sixth Patriarch of the Chan School. Afterwards, the four scrolls of the *Lankavatara Sutra* which had served as the basis of the Chan School since Bodhidharma arrived in China was now replaced by the *Diamond Sutra*. Therefore, for anyone wishing to understand the Chan School, Buddhism, or *prajna*, the *Diamond Sutra* is a great place to start.

In this day and age we usually strive for knowledge. All anyone has to do is open their eyes and they will be bombarded with massive amounts of information. Knowledge can help us analyze and understand the phenomena of the world. But even wisdom can have both a positive and a negative side. For example, Laozi, the ancient philosopher and founder of Daoism, once defined wisdom as "putting away sagacity and discarding wisdom," and we hear every day about people using their wisdom to commit crimes. Both of these cases show the possible negative and unwholesome aspects of wisdom. *Prajna*, on the other hand, is sought and developed from within our own minds, and transcends all knowledge and wisdom. This is why the word is not translated, and instead retains its Sanskrit pronunciation.

When I received full ordination at the age of fifteen, I got a taste of what it means to have to take the inhumane as humane, and the unreasonable as reasonable. My ordination master asked me whether I had killed any living beings. I answered, "No!"

Suddenly, a large willow branch struck me on the head.

"Am I to understand that you haven't killed any mosquitoes or ants?"

I quickly changed my answer, "Yes, I have."

Suddenly, the willow branch struck me again, because killing living beings is wrong. The ordination master then asked me whether my teacher had told me to come to the ordination ceremony. I answered, "I came on my own."

I was struck a third time.

"Your teacher didn't tell you to come? So you decide things all on your own? That deserves punishment!"

I accepted the reprimand with humility, and then answered, "It was my teacher who told me to come."

"So if he didn't tell you to come, you wouldn't have done so?"

Then I was struck for a fourth time.

I had to put up with quite a bit of pain and suffering during the fifty-three-day ordination period. For time to time, I would hear the sound of water or echoes from the mountain, and could not help wondering where it came from. When my ordination master saw that, he would swiftly strike me with a bamboo cane and say, "What are you listening to? Close your ears! Young as you are, what sounds belong to you?"

After being punished, I would quickly focus my mind. No matter how the wind blew and rustled the plants, I would hear none of it. The preceptor's bamboo cane then came down again.

"Open your ears and listen! What sound does not belong to you?"

Other times, I would receive a whack for casually looking around. My ordination master would say, "Your eyes are wandering! Can you see anything that belongs to you?"

When I was about to leave the monastery I saw how the wind was blowing across the grass and how the geese were soaring up through the clouds. I immediately caught myself and closed my eyes so as not to see, but my ordination master's cane was not going to let me off.

"Open your eyes and look around! What does not belong to you?"

If I gave a reason, I would get three whacks, but even if I gave no reason I would get three whacks. The willow branch had beaten away all pride and obstinacy and transformed me into a person who could act without a "self." When we think that we clearly understand something, know it in our heart, and that we've realized the Way, we end up with fixed ideas and preconceived notions about everything. We start to compare our knowledge and our practice with others, trying to see who comes out on top. This is when knowledge becomes an obstacle for us.

When we have been conditioned by knowledge and ideas, they can lead to attachments and arguments. Children are often unreasonable, and when defending some idea will say to other people: "That's what my dad says," or "that's what my mom says." They begin to change this after finishing kindergarten and move on to "That's what my teacher says." When they reach high school they say "That's what

my classmates say," and as young adults they change to "That's what
my boyfriend says" or "that's what my girlfriend says." After the age
of thirty or forty, they will gradually say things like "That's what
some spiritual teacher says," or "That's what some guru says." Now,
in the *Diamond Sutra*, the Buddha says:

 Subhuti, never say that the Tathagata has the thought,
"I have spoken the Dharma." Do not have that thought.
And why is this? If someone says that the Tathagata has
spoken the Dharma, then that person is defaming the
Buddha, and he does not understand what I have been
saying. Subhuti, when a person speaks the Dharma, no
Dharma can be spoken, and thus it is called speaking the
Dharma.

Why does the Buddha say that someone who says, "the Tathagata
has spoken the Dharma," then they are defaming the Buddha? The
Treatise on the Perfection of Great Wisdom says:

> The *prajna paramita* is divided into two aspects:
> its already realized aspect is called *bodhi*, while its
> yet unrealized aspect is called emptiness.

There are different degrees of "emptiness": a teacup is empty,
a house is also empty, and space too is empty. There is a Buddhist
saying that says "It is better to have a view of existence as grand
as Mount Sumeru, rather than give rise to a view of emptiness as
trifling as a mustard seed."

The sutras describe eighteen different aspects or levels of
emptiness, but some views of emptiness can become obstinate or

negative and result in nothing more than nihilism. It is better to not focus on "emptiness" as the object of spiritual study and practice. This concept is expanded upon in the following passage from the *Diamond Sutra*:

 Subhuti, suppose you had this thought: "It is not because his marks are complete that the Tathagata attains *anuttara samyaksambodhi.*" Subhuti, do not have this thought: "It is not because his marks are complete that the Tathagata attains *anuttara samyaksambodhi.*"

Subhuti, suppose you had this thought: "Those who initiate the mind of *anuttara samyaksambodhi* advocate the Dharma of annihilation." Do not have this thought. And why is this? Those who initiate the mind of *anuttara samyaksambodhi*, in regards to the Dharma, do not advocate the annihilation of notions.

"Advocating the Dharma of annihilation" means falling into having a one-sided and nihilistic view. Those who have their minds set upon supreme enlightenment (*anuttara samyaksambodhi*) "do not advocate the annihilation of notions." They do not cling to the notion of phenomena, nor do they cling to trying to get rid of such notions.

Prajna is the mother of all the Buddhas of the past, present, and future. It points directly to the original mind by piercing through all the various worldly afflictions and suffering such as the obstacles of language, knowledge, and ignorance. *Prajna* directly grasps the great wisdom of all the Buddhas and has a practical application in the present world. *Prajna* is truly life's secret ingredient for success.

Prajna is holding right view and being truly enlightened. *Prajna* is knowing that all phenomena arise through causes and conditions, and that they exist only temporarily. *Prajna* is understanding the inherent emptiness of dependent origination, and knowing that true emptiness is only possible because of wondrous existence. Emptiness does not dwell in emptiness, and existence does not abide within existence. The mind "that does not abide in anything," as mentioned in the *Diamond Sutra*, is the true mind with which all living beings are endowed. But *prajna* can only be bright and shining by experiencing it, observing it, and practicing it in daily life.

Earlier in my teaching career I divided *prajna* into four levels, based on the spiritual level of the practitioner. They are:

1. Right View
    Right View is the *prajna* of human and celestial beings; it is holding an opinion based on principles that are neither off track nor incorrect. It is like taking a photograph that shows one's own original face. Right view can come about from ordinary beings' understanding of cause and effect. Most people are able to learn through experience the causes and conditions for the ills of the world, such as illness, afflictions, monetary loss, and so on. Understanding cause and effect and thereby being able to be free from suffering is the worldly understanding of cause and effect.

2. Dependent Origination
    Dependent origination is the *prajna* of *sravakas* and *pratyekabuddhas*. Dependent origination can be

summarized as the doctrine that effects arise from causes, facts are founded upon principles, and that existence is established through emptiness—it is a supramundane teaching able to be comprehended by *sravakas, pratyekabuddhas,* and arhats. Such practitioners are able to ascertain that the five aggregates are empty, and so are free of mental hindrances. They have elevated their spirit to a higher level. They know all things and all affairs, and that there is nothing to do about them. They know that the sentient beings of the six realms of existence are all interconnected. They know that dependent origination is the true reality of the universe.

3. Emptiness

Emptiness is the *prajna* of bodhisattvas. Bodhisattvas do not only realize supramundane teachings, but the worldly teachings as well. Moreover, bodhisattvas take the next step and apply the transcendent mind to the conditions of this world. There is a verse that describes the *prajna* of the bodhisattva:

A color here, a fragrance there,
     are nothing but enlightenment's path;
Now speaking, now remaining silent,
     are all Chan in the end.

Use emptiness as one's causes and conditions, and naturally you will know all phenomena.

4. The Prajna of the Buddha

    The final level of the *prajna* of the Buddha is the state
    of non-duality between essence and phenomena at-
    tained after the *prajna* of one's own nature has been
    realized. In this state there is no division between
    transcendent teachings and worldly teachings, and all
    views of the self, others, and the outside world are
    eliminated. Causes and conditions may come and go,
    or may not come and go; there is no abiding in form.
    All things are perfectly and naturally integrated.

We can explain these four levels by how one learns to play
a musical instrument. Regardless of whether the instrument is a
flute, a violin, or a piano, when first learning to play, you must
start with reading music and fingering the strings or keys. Practice
comes by grasping at each note and each melody, going over each
note as indicated by the notation on the musical score. At this
stage you must look at the score before you play, just as one with
right view still relies on looking at the external world.

After practicing to a certain degree of fluency, the score has
already become ingrained in your mind, and you no longer need to
look at it to play. Although you do not look at the score any longer,
the score still exists within the mind, just as one who knows dependent origination has merely fused the internal and the external.

Continued diligent practice allows you to no longer look at the
score, nor consider it within your mind. At this point a piece of
music can be played straight through without any conscious effort
whatsoever with a performance that is seamless in all respects.
There is no longer a score inside or outside the mind, though the
"score" still remains as a cause; yet you still play according to the

score, as you are unable to create your own music. This is just as one who knows emptiness has left behind the internal and external.

Once you have mastered and integrated tonal modes and music theory, you can ride along with the great changes of the universe. You can now freely and effortlessly create music wherever the mind wanders or the spirit soars. This untrammeled mind is *prajna*; neither forgotten nor unforgotten. This is *prajna* at its highest level, with nothing internal and nothing external.

Right view, dependent origination, emptiness, and *prajna* are all "unconditioned Dharmas." There is a short Buddhist verse that explains what this means:

> Three kinds of birds fly through the sky;
> Their flight can be short or far;
> But the sky itself is neither short nor far.
> Three kinds of animals cross the river;
> Their crossing can be deep or shallow;
> But the water itself is neither deep nor shallow.

Consider the differences between a sparrow, pigeon, and eagle: some can fly for a short distance, and others for longer distances. Likewise if a rabbit, horse, and elephant were to cross a river, each would become submerged in the water differently because of their size. But the sky itself is neither short nor far, and the water is not shallow or deep. This analogy tells us that, while our realization of it may be shallow or deep, *prajna* itself is neither shallow nor deep. We should not become fixated upon what is shallow or deep. Do not fall into a nihilistic view.

The *Diamond Sutra* says that "all forms are illusory." People who are new to Buddhism can begin with an understanding of conditioned existence to lead up to an understanding that all forms are illusory. For us to understand the unconditioned teachings, we must first look at phenomena.

People often become confused by the illusory things outside the mind. Even if they are clearly illusions, we take them to be real. Even if they are clearly temporary, we cling to them desperately. This is why our mind abides in "existence" and becomes attached to externalities.

Those who become attached to rank and position will, in the end, find that it is lonely at the top. Those who become attached to fame and fortune will find themselves willing to die for the sake of wealth, as long as there is enough money involved. While it is okay to have anything in the world, whatever it may be, we must not become consumed with desire for it, for having excessive craving for something burdens us with caring for it and sorrow when it is gone. This is why we should look at everything in the world through the wisdom of *prajna*.

Prajna Is Everywhere in Life

How can we live lives that shine with the light of *prajna*? The opening of the *Diamond Sutra* describes how the Buddha manifests *prajna* in his daily routine of getting dressed and taking his meals. All living beings can experience and apply *prajna* in their daily activities, such as walking, standing, sitting, or lying down. As the Buddha ate, his mouth was illuminated; as he carried the alms bowl, his hands were illuminated; upon entering the city of Sravasti, his feet were illuminated; and as he sat in meditation, his whole body was illuminated. Each of these instances is a manifestation of wisdom and an example of *prajna*. The opening of the *Diamond Sutra* is as follows:

 Thus have I heard. At one time, the Buddha was in the city of Sravasti at the Jeta Grove Monastery with a gathering of monks numbering 1,250. At mealtime, the World-honored One put on his robe, picked up his bowl, and went into the city of Sravasti to beg for food. After he had gone from house to house, he returned to the grove. When he had finished eating, he put away his robe and bowl, washed his feet, straightened his mat, and sat down.

In this passage, the Venerable Ananda is recounting what he heard from the Buddha: At that time, the Buddha was dwelling in the Jeta Grove Monastery in the city of Sravasti, and there were twelve hundred and fifty monks attending to him there. When it was time to eat, the Buddha put on his monastic robe, and holding his alms bowl, he led his disciples into the city of Sravasti to gather alms from house to house. Afterwards, he returned to the Jeta Grove Monastery. After finishing his meal, the Buddha put his robe and bowl away, washed his feet, spread out his mat, and then sat in a cross-legged position.

Let us take a closer look at the how the Buddha exemplifies the six *paramitas* through his carefree daily routine, depicted in the opening of the *Diamond Sutra*:

1. The Buddha demonstrates the *paramita* of morality when he "put on his robe, [and] picked up his bowl," showing the calm solemnity of how he observed the rules of proper behavior.

2.   The Buddha demonstrates the *paramita* of giving when he gathers alms in the city. By going out to gather alms, the Buddha enables living beings to hear the Dharma. The Buddha thus makes a connection with living beings by giving the gift of the Dharma.

3.   The Buddha demonstrates the *paramita* of patience by gathering alms "from house to house." Going to each house shows that the Buddha does not care whether his bowl is full or empty, or whether the food is good or bad. Everything is treated equally.

4.   The Buddha demonstrates the *paramita* of diligence when he "had finished eating, he put away his robe and bowl." From entering the city to beg for food to the putting away of his robe, the Buddha relied upon no one else.

5.   The Buddha demonstrates the *paramita* of meditative concentration when it is said that he "washed his feet, straightened his mat, and sat down."

6.   This one day in the life of the Buddha, from dressing and eating to feet washing and mat spreading, completes the five *paramitas*. These aspects of daily life are the external manifestations of the "form" of the *paramita* of *prajna*, while the essence of *prajna* itself is found within the mind. When the mind of *prajna* is applied to all the activities of daily life, this fulfills the *paramita* of *prajna*.

In the opening of the *Diamond Sutra,* the Buddha embodies the life of the six *paramitas,* shining with the light of *prajna.* He does not display supernatural powers with conjuring tricks, but rather wants us to live a life of *prajna* by using the *prajna* within our own minds in our ordinary, everyday lives.

Prajna is like light, for light is unsullied, pure, and carefree. To be illuminated by the light of *prajna* is not something only for the Buddhas and bodhisattvas. As long as we speak tender, kind, and encouraging words, are our mouths not illuminated? When we observe the world and look at all living beings equally with compassionate eyes and contemplate society with the eyes of wisdom, are our eyes not illuminated? When we are able to serve others with the labor of our own hands, are the palms of our hands not illuminated? When we listen to the Dharma and chanting in praise of the Buddha, are our ears not illuminated? When our faces are smiling with compassion and kindness, are our faces not illuminated? When our minds are full of compassion, *bodhi,* and a commitment to the path, are our minds not illuminated? When we properly observe decorum and have a calming countenance in all of our actions, maintaining a nonjudgmental attitude towards the cruelty and corruption of others, are our whole bodies not illuminated?

When people reach a stage where their light no longer shines, they are like a lantern painted black. We should not just be concerned with external things like sunlight, electric lights, lamplight, and firelight, nor should we take notice of the dim, false lights within perverse and misleading ideas. The most important question to ask is: Where is our light? Can our eyes, ears, nose, tongue, and body all be illuminated? Is it possible for our mind to shine forth with light? Can we light the mental lamp of our intrinsic nature and the truth of *prajna?*

The *Original Vows of Ksitigarbha Bodhisattva Sutra* states: "Be humble and smiling, and personally perform acts of giving everywhere." All the Buddhas and bodhisattvas create the causes and conditions needed to liberate all sentient beings. They must be as humble as the ground, and personally perform acts of giving with a smile. Practicing in this way means living a life of *prajna* such that everyone can be peaceful, carefree, and at ease.

Putting Prajna into Practice

No one can live your life or become enlightened for you. But how is it that *prajna* is inherent to the mind? How can we attain enlightenment and see our nature? We should not rely on holy water, magical talismans, or the empowerments and blessings of a guru, for we must break through the delusions within. In all things you must depend upon yourself. There is no one else who can take your place.

Once Xiangyan Zhixian had come to study with Chan Master Weishan Lingyou. Lingyou said, "I have heard that at Chan Master Baizhang Huaihai's place you gave ten answers for every question and a hundred answers for every ten. Is this true?"

Zhixian answered, "It is, I'm ashamed to say."

Lingyou continued, "That's nothing more than clever worldly repartee. It will be no help whatsoever in liberating you from the cycle of birth and death. Now I ask you, what was your original face before you were born?"

Zhixian pondered the matter for a long while, and then he asked for instruction, "Master, please be compassionate and teach me."

Lingyou replied, "I know that if I were to reveal the answer to you now, you would curse me in the future when you truly attain enlightenment."

If in learning Buddhism we only chase after profound spiritual experiences or only request the teacher's instructions to help us avoid trouble, then we have wasted our mental effort. It is no different from watching an athlete train as we sit by on the sidelines; by only watching, we will not become any stronger or more agile. Any specialty requires its own systematic training, so if we wish to live a life of wisdom, how can we ever act conceited or lazy?

Once Chan Master Daoqian and his good friend Zongyuan were traveling on foot, walking to various monasteries to learn from the great Chan masters. As they journeyed, Zongyuan found the mountain and river crossings extremely difficult and tiring, so on many occasions, he complained and demanded to end their trip.

Finally, Daoqian comforted him and said, "We have decided to take this tour to study and learn, and it would be a shame to abandon it in the middle of our trip. I know you are very weary and tired, but from now on I will do whatever I can do for you. However, there are five tasks that I cannot help you with."

"What five?" Zongyuan asked.

Daoqian smiled, "Getting dressed, eating meals, urinating, defecating, and walking."

Zongyuan then understood what Daoqian was talking about. There was more that Daoqian could not do for him than just getting dressed, eating meals, urinating, defecating, and walking. It is truly impossible for other people to live your life for you. So if you truly wish to live a life of wisdom, how can you slack off and rely on others?

There are some people who have been faithful Buddhists for many years and have delved into the Buddhist sutras and who can talk a great deal about the principles in those Buddhist books, but they are incapable of applying the teachings to their lives. Such people cannot let go of who is right or wrong and who wins or loses. This goes against the essence of the *Diamond Sutra.* If Buddhism becomes separated from life, there can be no *prajna,* nor can there be any understanding of "emptiness."

Once there was a businessman who considered himself to be a Buddhist, but he suffered from a terrible temper. When angered, he would curse and shout at his own mother without realizing what he was saying. One day, he went to the Buddhist temple to light some incense, and there he saw a statue of Avalokitesvara Bodhisattva, splendid and majestic. The businessman thought, "It is said that Avalokitesvara Bodhisattva responds to every request, so if I were able to see the bodhisattva for myself, I could ask for my business to prosper and my work to go well, and I will make even more money."

The businessman then spoke to the abbot of the temple asking, "Venerable, how can I see Avalokitesvara Bodhisattva for myself?"

The abbot thought he could free the businessman of his delusions, so he said to him, "Return home: if you see someone wearing their clothes backwards and having put their shoes on wrong, then that person is the very Avalokitesvara Bodhisattva who responds to every request."

Overjoyed, the businessman hurried back home, but along the way he saw no bodhisattva as described by the abbot. He became furious with the venerable abbot for having deceived him, so when he finally returned home, he knocked on the door with great force. His mother heard the urgent knocking, and came to the door shaken and in great haste. As a result she had gotten dressed so quickly that her clothes were on backwards and she had put her shoes on the wrong way.

The door opened and the businessman saw his mother—was this not Avalokitesvara Bodhisattva as described by the abbot? The businessman realized the error of his ways and felt regret. His mother, who had suckled him as a baby and spent her whole life devoted to looking after him, was she not a bodhisattva who responds to every request? From then on the businessman changed; he took care of his mother with respect and devotion all the rest of her days.

Prajna is not present only when reciting the *Diamond Sutra*, nor is it necessarily present during retreat. *Prajna* exists in the ordinary, everyday activities of eating and dressing; it is present in how one deals with the world and the people and things in it.

Longtan Chongxin went to study with Chan Master Tianhuang Daowu. Longtan Chongxin stayed with the Chan master for twenty years, yet during that time he did not feel that he had gained a great understanding of the Dharma.

Finally Longtan went before Chan Master Tianhuang Daowu to ask to leave the monastery. Chan Master Tianhuang asked, "Where are you going?"

Longtan said, "I will travel around to learn and study the Dharma."

"The Dharma is right here. Where else would you go to learn?"

"I've been here over a dozen years now and have never heard you give me any instruction in the Dharma. How can the Dharma be here?"

"How could you lie like that!" Chan Master Tianhuang continued, "What do you mean there's no Dharma here? You bring tea every day and I receive it from you and drink it. Then you bring food and I receive it from you and eat it. You join your palms together and bow, while I nod my head. In every one of these instances I am teaching you the Dharma. How could the Dharma not be here? These things are the Dharma. They are the *prajna* of everyday life!"

Longtan said, "Oh. That's *prajna*? Let me think about it."

Chan Master Tianhuang replied, "You can't think about it; thinking is the discriminating mind and that's not *prajna*."

From hearing these words Longtan finally understood.

Such teachings are truly beyond conception and show moments of sudden realization. In the *Mind Seal Commentary to the Diamond Sutra*, the great Qing dynasty scholar Puwan commented upon this passage from the *Diamond Sutra*:

> At that time the elder monk Subhuti was among the gathering of monks. He rose from his seat, bore his right shoulder, knelt on his right knee, and with palms pressed together before him, respectfully spoke to the Buddha saying...

With the verse:

> In a fiery transformation
>   and a churning of waves,
>   a dragon is born;
> While the shrimps and crabs
>   merely exert their eyes.

Puwan explained how enlightened people are like dragons that can fly through the sky, riding the wind and rain, while those who have yet to attain enlightenment are like shrimps or crabs that can only exert their eyes, giving a stirring description of the ignorance of the unenlightened.

That opportunity for sudden realization is present throughout our lives. Every day there are opportunities for enlightenment. People who are too tired to get out of bed and suffer the daily frustrations of being late may come to the sudden realization that they should get up earlier. People who are weak may come to the sudden realization that they should start to exercise daily. But these are so often just passing thoughts, for ingrained habits are hard to change. Buddhist enlightenment is not the same as a momentary realization. It must be experienced in our lives and practiced in our daily activities. This is the only way to experience Chan in daily life, for Chan *is* daily life. Only by putting our realizations into practice can we gradually be freed from our affliction and suffering and attain the freedom of *bodhi*.

The *Miscellaneous Treasures Sutra* tells the story of the mutual hatred between a maidservant and a goat: Once there was a maidservant who was responsible for working in the mill. Each morning she would take coarse grains and pulses, like barley and soy, that her master had given her and grind them into meal. However, a certain goat would often steal a bite of the soy meal whenever the maidservant was not looking. For this reason the master often suspected that the maidservant was not making enough soy meal, so he would berate her and punish her with a beating. Each time after the maidservant was punished by the master, she would angrily take up a bamboo stick and beat the goat. Being beaten repeatedly, the goat grew increasingly spiteful, as well.

One day, the maidservant was making a fire and the goat saw that there was no bamboo stick in her hand, so he butted her with his horns. The maidservant became angry and flustered, so she picked up a burning piece of firewood and beat the goat. The goat's flesh began to burn, and he was in great pain, dashing madly about and throwing sparks from his flaming body, spreading the fire to the nearby villagers and their homes. The blaze grew and even consumed the surrounding mountains and wild plains. Five hundred monkeys who were living on the mountain could not escape the blaze, and they, too, perished in the fire.

Such a terrible disaster all came from the anger and hatred between the goat and the maidservant. It is from instances like this that the Buddhist saying, "The flames of anger can burn up a forest of merit" comes from. Anger can make us feel as though we have plunged into a land of demons with rancid winds and rains of blood.

The *Upasaka Precepts Sutra* states that there are three kinds of enlightenment:

> One kind is attained through hearing; the second kind is attained through contemplation; and the third kind is attained through cultivation. Since the *sravakas* have attained enlightenment by hearing [the Buddha's teachings], they are not called Buddhas; since the *pratyekabuddhas* have attained their own partial realization through contemplation, they are called *pratyekabuddhas*. The Tathagata has no teacher and attains enlightenment through cultivation and not through reliance upon hearing or contemplation. This is total enlightenment, and so such a person is called the Buddha.

The Tathagata is the Buddha not because of hearing the Dharma or contemplating it; rather, the Buddha attains enlightenment through the process of cultivating the Dharma. This is why such a person can become the Buddha.

Once there was a man who made a living as a thief. One day, his son said to him, "Dad, you are getting old. How am I to make a living? You really ought to pass on to me the secrets of your trade."

The father said, "Fine. I will pass on my knowledge to you tonight."

When the still hours of the night arrived, the father told his son to go out with him. Soon they found a house and prepared to break in. The two jumped over the wall and entered the house. Once inside, the father opened a cupboard, and told his son to hide himself within. Suddenly, the father started shouting:

"Thief! Thief! There's a thief here!"

The father's shouting woke the homeowner, who immediately came down to catch the thief. By then the elder thief had run away, but his son was still hiding in the closed cupboard. The young thief thought to himself: "How could my father do such a thing? Why did he shut me up in this cupboard and then run off after shouting an alarm? What am I going to do now?" The only thing he could do was look for a way to get out of this predicament on his own.

Desperation is the mother of invention, and so the young thief came up with an idea: Still inside the cupboard, he started to imitate the sound of a mouse:

"Squeak, squeak, squeak."

The homeowner was looking for the thief with a candle in hand, and when he heard the mouse squeaking, he relaxed.

"Oh, it's only a mouse. The thief must have run off."

When he had let his guard down, the young thief dashed out of the cupboard and blew out the candle. In the darkness, the homeowner ran after the thief. The young thief was quite worried now, and the chase was on.

The young thief then thought of another idea: he ran by an old well, picked up a large stone, and threw it in. When the homeowner reached the well he said, "Alas, it looks like this well claimed somebody's life tonight."

The homeowner then left. The young thief was able to return home safe and sound.

When he arrived home, the young thief found his father, and took him to task: "Why did you play such a trick on me today?"

The father asked, "What do you mean I 'played a trick' on you?"

"I mean closing me up in a cupboard and then shouting, 'Thief! Thief!'"

The father then asked, "So, how did you get out of it?"

The son told him everything that happened. The father was very pleased and said:

"Son, I have found my successor in you. Now you understand. You know that to adapt to changing circumstances you must depend upon yourself. Others cannot pass on anything to us!"

We often hear about students blaming their teachers for favoritism, disciples blaming their spiritual mentors for not passing on the "real secrets," and children blaming their parents for the partiality of their love. But success and fulfillment are not things that others can give us. *Prajna* is inherent to our own minds; it is one's will to succeed and the power to put one's vision into practice. If we do not seek *prajna* within, nor practice *prajna* in our lives and, instead, only indulge in idle talk of *prajna*, what good does it do?

When Fifth Patriarch Hongren passed on the robe and bowl to Huineng, he knew that initially no one in the monastic community would understand, so he had Huineng leave the monastery at Huangmei in the middle of the night. After departing from Huangmei, several hundred monastics chased after Huineng to try and claim the robe and alms bowl. One such monastic, Huiming, was the first to catch up with him, and tried to take the robe and bowl that had been given to Huineng by the Fifth Patriarch.

Huineng laid the robe and bowl on a rock beside the road and said, "This robe symbolizes trust. How can you take it by force?"

Huineng then hid away among the bushes. When Huiming tried to take the robe and bowl, he found that he could not lift them, and then he understood. He felt ashamed of himself and then begged Sixth Patriarch Huineng to give him instruction in the Dharma.

Huineng said, "Remove all your mental conditioning and do not give rise to a single thought. [...] Do not think of wholesomeness. Do not think of unwholesomeness."

Huiming then asked, "Besides the hidden and profound meaning imparted to me now, is there any other?"

Huineng answered, "If I could tell you, it would not be hidden. If you reflect within, the hidden and profound are close at hand."

The true hidden meaning is to eliminate the place where thoughts dwell, and cut off the path of language. *Prajna*, pure and free, is right here in our minds. But even if one has grasped this hidden meaning and has attained *prajna*, it is still up to us to carry it through in the actual practice of daily life in a dynamic and adaptive fashion.

Fostering Executive Power

The ability to get things done and accomplish one's vision is the secret that can bring success to any organization or enterprise. In Chinese, we call this *zhixing li* (執行力), "the power to execute." One example of *zhixing li* was, towards the end of 1996, Fo Guang Shan took less than three months to arrange in good order the holding of an international colloquium for Catholic and Buddhist leaders. Cardinal Francis Arinze was surprised, and the impression we made was quite profound. After being informed of this event, the late Pope John Paul II looked forward to later meeting me.

As long as we believe in the power of the mind, we can take each day and look on the bright side, thinking of how each matter will be successful and how we can make it a success. Every day we can open our eyes and feel hopeful. If we work in this way unceasingly, we will surely be successful.

The failure of worldly enterprise often comes from conditions not being right. Success comes from being able to develop the right conditions. That is the greatest secret to success in life. It is commonly said throughout the Buddhist teachings that "all phenomena arise through causes and conditions." This means that any business undertaking requires the proper conditions of capital, land, markets, planning, publicity, qualified personnel, and so on. If any one of these conditions is lacking, then the undertaking will not easily succeed. For this reason there is no need to play the blame game when difficulties appear. It is important to create connections with others, and remain focused on people. That is the only way to get along well in the world, and only by getting along with others can we create the wide-ranging connections to bring about a better future. When we take the initiative to dedicate our abilities to others, we align ourselves with new and different causes and conditions, allowing us to be successful when we have the right conditions in the future.

It is possible to accomplish many things under difficult circumstances, but in my own life, I've never felt I've had to face difficult circumstances. What other people did not dare consider I have always been willing to try, and I did not give up when encountering setbacks. Instead I waited for the right conditions, or tried to create the necessary positive conditions. Once I had made a decision to do something, I would then explain the necessity and importance of the undertaking to my disciples, and I was not easily dissuaded by the majority's opposition.

Before launching the *Merit Times* in 2000, the senior journalist Lu Keng came to Fo Guang Shan to see me. Some of his friends had told him, "You have to convince the master that trying to launch a Buddhist-run newspaper is impossible. He must not do it under any circumstances."

As we talked, not only did it turn out that Lu Keng was unable to disabuse me of my plan, but I even talked him into writing his own column for the *Merit Times*.

When I was young I developed the habit of thinking things out. I would think, "If I had the chance to start a magazine, how would I organize all its content?" or, "If I had the chance to spread the Dharma, what and how would I teach?" I never waited around idly or became hesitant or pessimistic when conditions were not right for action. I listened attentively, and through the process of giving without notions, I learned from everyone I encountered, accumulating experience and wisdom. Once the right conditions were present, I was already well prepared with all the necessary planning, procedures, and details, regardless of whether I was building a temple or founding a school, so naturally these projects were able to progress smoothly.

Whenever the Buddha taught the Dharma, six conditions needed to be present: the right faith, right listening, right time, right teacher, right place, and right audience. These six conditions can be seen in the opening line of the *Diamond Sutra*: "Thus have I heard. At one time, the Buddha was in the city of Sravasti at the Jeta Grove Monastery with a gathering of monks numbering 1,250." The six conditions are as follows:

Thus	**Faith:** In order to be able to receive the teaching the faith of the assembly should already be established.
have I heard	**Listening:** The members of the assembly should already possess the necessary merit to hear the teachings.
at one time	**Time:** The time to deliver the teachings has ripened.
the Buddha	**Teacher:** The master delivering the teaching joyfully teaches the wondrous Dharma.
city of Sravasti at the Jeta Grove	**Location:** The venue that the teachings are being delivered in is suitable.
gathering of monks numbering 1,250	**Audience:** The faithful assembly that is ready to hear the teachings has gathered together.

These six right conditions must be present in order for a Dharma teaching to occur. Even now, our reading of the *Diamond Sutra* is made possible due to exceptional circumstances. We should all be thankful for the causes and conditions in the world that have enabled our existence, and we should be thankful to others who have contributed to our success. This is something truly worthy of joyous praise. Everything that is or has happened in the universe is a product of causes and conditions.

No Buddhist sutra ever clarifies the date or time that a certain teaching is given, instead simply using the expression *yishi* (一時), "at one time." Why are there no clear indications of time given in the sutras? Because what we understand as "time" is merely due to the differences in how living beings experience the effects of their karma. For example, the time in each country on the globe is not the same: When it is 1:00 P.M. in Taiwan it is still the predawn hour in the United States. Our planet has many different regions, which is why we perceive this "time difference." The expression "at one time" found in the sutras eliminates this limited concept of time and space that living beings have. As long as we are of the same mind as the Buddha, then the phrase "at one time" is like a limitless benefit that is everlasting.

The *Dirgha Agama* tells the story about blowing a conch shell that can act as a metaphor for how causes and conditions work together. A long time ago there were people living in a village who had never heard the sound made by blowing a conch shell. One day, a young man who knew how to play a conch came to this village. He took out a conch shell, blew into it three times and put it on the ground.

When the villagers heard the sound they were amazed. They rushed towards the man from all directions, and asked, "How did you make such a nice, pleasant sound?"

The young man pointed to the conch shell and said, "This is what made the sound."

The villagers touched the conch shell with their hands and spoke to it saying, "Would you please make that wonderful sound again?"

But the conch shell remained silent. The young man picked up the conch shell again and blew into it three more times. It was only then that the villagers realized what was going on. One of them spoke up and said, "That beautiful, pleasing sound is not the work of the conch shell. That man's hands, mouth, and breath must work in concert with it before the conch shell makes its sound."

The highest level of management is the management of the mind. Fo Guang Shan built its massive organization through faith in Humanistic Buddhism. In Buddhism, we commonly use the expression *faxin* (發心), "arouse the mind," which means to generate an aspiration to do something. The formation of Fo Guang Shan's monastic and lay orders came about through collective creativity in which each individual *faxin*, generated the aspiration for compassion and dedicated their efforts, physical and mental, to accomplishing the goal. This was not something that any one individual could accomplish alone. Since the faith in Humanistic Buddhism benefits living beings and allows us a joy that is blameless, everyone is willing to participate no matter what hardships must be faced.

Consider Fo Guan Shan's use of money. There is a saying in Fo Guang Shan that "what comes from the ten directions, goes out to the ten directions," meaning that donations from around the world are distributed around the world, not just in a temple's locality. Every penny comes from the generosity of living beings, so the money must be used in the best possible way for activities or special projects with every attempt being made to come in under budget. Fo Guang Shan's many volunteers and staff are another example. Given its common sense of purpose, many people are willing to generate the aspiration to commit their physical and mental effort, so long as what they do benefits the needs of the whole. Many private enterprises cannot achieve such a feat. But this is liberation with no notion of self.

The words *faxin* do not explicitly appear in the *Diamond Sutra*, so many people think that the importance of generating aspiration is not mentioned in the text. However, the sutra does say:

> Of all sentient beings, be they born of eggs, wombs, moisture, or transformation, or whether they have form, or not form, or whether they are able to perceive, or do not perceive, or are neither able to perceive or not perceive, I cause them to enter *nirvana* without remainder, liberating them.

This certainly describes generating an aspiration. Generating the aspiration to help so many living beings does not mean receiving the merit that comes from giving them food to eat or clothes to wear. Rather, it means enabling living beings to be liberated. Hence the line that follows: "Thus...liberating infinite, immeasurable, limitless sentient beings."

The Buddha did not think that living beings were liberated by him, because living beings are intrinsically Buddhas. The Buddha was simply granting them liberation in accordance with causes and conditions. The Buddha does not claim any merit, nor does he abide in merit. This indeed is "generating aspiration," that is, generating expansive aspiration, generating impartial aspiration, generating non-deluded aspiration, generating egalitarian aspiration, and generating universal aspiration. Truly this is a great aspiration without limitation!

When I was seventeen, I contracted malaria. Every day I would shift between fever and chills; it was quite unbearable. The other students at the Buddhist college would entrust their lives to the celestial beings who protect the Dharma, and would simply weather any hardship. I never heard anyone ask to rest, even when they were sick, so I dragged my sick and weakened body through to the work and rest periods along with all the others, and then collapsed into my bed each night. After about a month of this, my teacher, the Venerable Zhikai, had someone bring me a half bowl of pickled vegetables. Holding that bowl of pickled vegetables with both hands, tears streamed down my face. I was grateful to my teacher for caring for me in this way. At the moment I vowed: "For as long as I live, I will dedicate all of my mind and body to Buddhism without fail, so as to repay the kindness of my teacher."

Soon afterward, my illness was completely cured.

In order to promote Buddhism, I have never refrained from reinventing myself. Even when conditions were not right, I did not simply sit idly by waiting for the right conditions to appear. Sometimes, in order to turn things around, we have to assemble forces from all directions, create momentum, and exert influence. The Buddha did not attempt to change others externally, rather he tried to change himself internally. I have tried to emulate the Buddha's revolutionary spirit within, so that I could change my own ideas, eliminate bad habits, and renew myself unceasingly.

One must be a sponge: never stop soaking up learning and assimilating new things. Do not be like a plastic bag that even a drop of water cannot penetrate.

A Person's Unlimited Potential

I have always been shy by nature, and from a young age I invariably became tongue-tied when speaking to groups. Consequently, if I had to appear on stage, I would read my speech over and over again beforehand until I knew it by heart. I would also take an active role in receiving guests at the monastery, and would think about how to answer their possible questions beforehand. Late into the night I would always spend some time reflecting upon the successes and failures with my conversations that day, no matter how exhausted I was.

My intelligence, ability, and wisdom are no better than other people's. When I was studying at the Buddhist college, I took the reprimands from the teachers and the derision of my classmates as right and proper, and I vowed to make up for my deficiencies through physical labor. I would get out of bed early, groping in the dark, so that I could be up to beat the wooden blocks, signaling the other monastics to start their day. While my classmates were studying on their own, I would volunteer to go to the river and fetch water for the monastic community. Before and after our meals I would rush over to the kitchen and living quarters to sweep up. I would spend any free time apart from my studies by heading over to the kitchen to cook, so I was constantly going back and forth amid all the firewood, rice, oil, and salt in the kitchen and its stoves of boiling water.

During the ten years I lived at my training monastery, I worked as a server in the dining hall for six years, spent two years fetching water for the monastery, and another year and a half tending to the main shrine, taking care of the lamps, incense, images, and offerings. During this time I also served as administrator for the monastery library. Working in the dining hall was the hardest: each year when winter came around both my hands would be soaking in cold water as I washed several hundred sets of bowls and chopsticks. The skin on both the palms and the back of my hands were chapped all over, exposing raw, red skin between the cracks.

To train my mind and body and stimulate my potential, I emulated the great monastics of the past by undergoing various kinds of austere practices. I practiced not eating after noon so that I could directly experience the spiritual joy of transcending the desire to satisfy my appetite. I transcribed the sutras using my own blood to make a flesh-and-blood connection between myself and the Buddha, and forge a mental connection with living beings. When the monastery enforced periods of silence, I would slap myself if I violated the prohibition and, over time, I would no longer engage in idle gossip even within my own mind. When paying homage to the Buddha as an act of penance, I would bow before the Buddha, kneeling for a long time repenting for my past lifetimes of negative karma so that my ignorance could be peeled away layer by layer.

Most people who pray are seeking something for themselves. Before the age of twenty I was the same: I would always pray to the Buddha to bless me, and ask that he ensure I become intelligent and make good progress, and that I be able to break through any difficulty and master the Buddhist path. After the age of twenty, after I had graduated from the Buddhist college, I came to feel that all I had been doing was praying to the Buddhas and bodhisattvas on my own behalf, asking for this and that. Wasn't that selfish? Afterwards, I prayed instead for my parents and teachers, my relatives and companions, and even for those devotees with whom

I felt especially connected, wishing that they would be safe and sound, and that they would grow in happiness and wisdom.

As I entered my forties, I gradually began to reflect upon my life and realized that my prayers still constituted a kind of selfish desire. Thus, between the ages of forty and fifty, I began praying for world peace, for a strong and prosperous nation, for a peaceful and happy society, and for the liberation of living beings.

After I turned fifty I had another insight. I was beseeching the Buddhas and bodhisattvas every single day to bring about peace and happiness for the world, for society, and for living beings, but what was I supposed to be doing about it? Thus, after the age of fifty, I began to pray to the Buddhas and bodhisattvas to let me shoulder the burden of the karmic obstacles and sufferings of all living beings: allow me to take on all the bitter transience of human emotions, allow me to practice the great compassion of the Buddha, and allow me to learn how to demonstrate the benefits and joy of the Dharma like the Buddha.

Prajna is concerned with both realization and attainment. The realization of enlightenment is not the same as the attainment of enlightenment. One who realizes can be in accordance with the truth, but such a realization is still not perfect. What attainment of the highest truth looks like can be seen in the story of the meeting between Emperor Wu of the Liang dynasty and the great Chan patriarch, Bodhidharma. Emperor Wu asked, "All my life, I have built temples, sponsored monastics, practiced generosity, and made food offerings. What virtue have I gained?"

Bodhidharma answered, "In truth, there is no virtue"

Bodhidharma's understanding of merit and virtue was different from Emperor Wu's. Did Emperor Wu have any merit? Of course he did; he had mundane, worldly merit. There is always some merit or virtue gained, no matter how much or how little is done. But mundane virtue cannot compare to ultimate virtue for those of great ability that is unconditioned and beyond attainment; such virtue pervades heaven and earth. What Bodhidharma was talking about was the virtue of intrinsic nature. That is what we seek so assiduously. In modern terms we would call this "discovering our unlimited potential," like martial artists who become stronger as their skills reach a higher level, and as in gongfu novels when the heroes open up their *qi* channels.

Nowadays I sometimes hear people talk about how great Fo Guang Shan is. But I will counter: Great in what way? The number of temples or how large the organization has developed arises naturally in accordance with conditions. While I began learning Buddhism well before the age of seventy, one could say that such learning did not mature until I became seventy. Many of the principles have been with me all this time, it was just that before I saw them only vaguely and just kept going towards what I wanted at that moment. Being carefree is not something we can search for. Finding the intrinsic nature of the true, *prajna* mind is the process of becoming more carefree, and that happens day by day.

Buddhist sutras always begin with the words "thus I have heard" and conclude with the words "they believed, received, and practiced it." Being able to believe in, receive, and practice the Dharma is "acting like a Buddha." To act like a Buddha is much closer to the Buddha's aim than understanding Dharma knowledge or memorizing the Buddhist texts. Acting like a Buddha means putting the Buddha's teaching into actual practice. We typically call Buddhists "practitioners," because they are "practicing" the Dharma, that is, acting as the Buddha said and did. A true practitioner must act like the Buddha, not merely "study Buddhism." If one wants to attain any success, one has to live in the practice every moment of every day and in every place. We should not learn some skillful teaching only to lay it aside and forget about it.

We read the *Diamond Sutra* in order to act like a Buddha in daily life and to apply the sutra's teachings to the real world in a practical way. Whether or not we are successful, whether or not we can find fulfillment, then becomes a question of whether or not we can live a life that is carefree with *prajna* and a diamond-like mind.

III

Vajra

Destroyer of Affliction

Allow me to begin with a story: once upon a time there lived an old woman who would chant the name of Amitabha Buddha from morning to night, so much so that people called her "Old Amitofo Chanter." After her death, she appeared before Yama, the lord of death and judge of the hell realm.

Yama took one look at the old woman and said, "Send her to the hell realm!"

The old woman protested, "In life I was called 'Old Amitofo Chanter' and you're sending me off to hell? Surely you have made a mistake!"

"My judgments are never wrong, but I'll prove it to you. Demons, go check again."

Yama's demons wheeled out eight large wagons full of all the merit from the old woman's recitations of Amitabha Buddha's name, dumped them into a wicker scoop, and gave them a shake. As the demons shook them, all the old woman could hear was a series of cracks as all her merit broke into pieces. All of her recitations were now a jumble of scraps, for there was no merit in them.

"You see?" Yama said. "There are no solid karmic rewards among the Amitabha Buddha recitations you did in life."

At that moment, a red demon exclaimed, "Lord Yama, there is one left!"

Only one unbroken bit of merit remained, and it had come about in the following way: on one occasion the old woman was on her way to the temple to bow to the Buddha when she was overtaken by a rainstorm and a bolt of lightning that struck a fir tree standing right in front of her. In that instant the old woman's mind was free of distraction and did not abide in anything, at which point she recited "Namo Amitofo" (Taking refuge in Amitabha Buddha). It was only this particular recitation of Amitabha Buddha's name that remained as merit after she passed away, allowing her to escape the suffering of hell.

There is a similar story about a man named "Stone Hui." Stone Hui's family had been stonemasons for generations, which is why people called him "Stone Hui." Stone Hui was illiterate, but he would still ask the Buddhist monks to recite the sutras for him. Having listened to them so many times, he was also able to recite some from memory as well.

Later on, Stone Hui left his family and went to Chan Master Dasui's temple to work as a manual laborer, where he was assigned the task of chiseling stone. His iron hammer never left his hand, and his lips never stopped reciting the Buddhist sutras.

Chan Master Dasui would see him work like this every day, and finally asked, "You're tap tapping today, and you'll be tap tapping tomorrow; what will you do when you are at death's door?"

Stone Hui cast aside his iron hammer and followed Dasui into the abbot's chambers. Dasui wanted him to stop memorizing

Buddhist sutras and give up his attachment to the written word.

One day, Stone Hui was chiseling stone once more, and the stone he was working on was exceedingly hard. He struck forcefully at the stone with all his might. Sparks flew everywhere, and there amid all the sparks, Stone Hui suddenly attained enlightenment. Afterwards he entered the abbot's chambers, paid homage to Chan Master Dasui, and spoke the following verse:

> Exhausting all my effort,
> Completely forgetting myself,
> In a burst of flying sparks,
> Here it is all along.

Dasui realized that Stone Hui was now enlightened, and consequently bestowed upon him a set of monastic robes.

Stone Hui then entered the Dharma hall to teach, and said: "If you are unclear about your own mind while practicing meditation and learning the Way, then you are like a person crying out in thirst while being inside a well. Within a day we walk, stand, sit, and lie down; we are always moving and doing, is there anything that is not changing? The eyes see and the ears hear, so where is the path not present? If you can recognize the path, that is the path of great liberation. Look at me. I'm an old man: am I better than you in any way? Is there any way you are inferior? Understand? The moon is reflected within the waves across the 36,000 acres of Lake Tai. To whom is it speaking?"

After he finished speaking, Stone Hui got up and left.

To go through the motions of reciting sutras and bowing to the Buddha without putting your heart into it is a total waste of time, no matter how much effort is involved. Such unmindful practices will not help your life in any way. After listening to the Dharma we must think about, practice, and realize the teachings to attain enlightenment. We must rediscover our minds. The mind is *prajna*, also called *vajra*. *Vajra* is a Sanskrit word, translated as *jingang* (金剛) in Chinese, which describes a material that is sharp and powerful, often translated as "diamond." The mind itself is very powerful and has limitless potential. When we rediscover the mind, it becomes like a diamond, sharp and powerful, and absolutely true without illusions. Such a mind grants right understanding and allows us to see the truth.

The Diamond Is Prajna

People have as many distracting thoughts as there are specks of dust in the universe. The Buddha understands the character and habits of living beings, and like a sharp, diamond blade cuts away at the distracting, delusional thoughts that bind our minds. This allows us to go directly to our inherent mind and no longer be dazzled and confused by worldly phenomena.

In the *Diamond Sutra* the Buddha teaches the wondrous Dharma that can grind away at our ignorance and delusion within and without. The diamond is used as a symbol for *prajna*, infinitely durable and sharp. The Buddha teaches us that we have always possessed this treasure within ourselves, and that we can use it to cut away our affliction and ignorance and attain the wisdom of the Dharmakaya within our intrinsic nature.

The diamond represents the *prajna* of our intrinsic nature and the Chan mind. In Buddhism, it is said that "all Buddhas are always liberating the sentient beings within our minds," referring to the thoughts and afflictions we all carry. However, the wondrous thing that *prajna* can do is to allow sentient beings to always partake of the intrinsic nature of all Buddhas. *Prajna* is everyone's inherent, limitless potential.

All Forms Are Illusory

At that time, Subhuti asked the Buddha, "World-honored One, what should this sutra be called, and how should we receive it and uphold it?"

The Buddha said to Subhuti, "This sutra is called the *Diamond Prajnaparamita*, and by this name you should receive it and uphold it. And why is this? Subhuti, the Buddha has said that *prajnaparamita* is not *prajnaparamita* and that that is what is called *prajnaparamita*. Subhuti, what do you think? Does the Tathagata speak the Dharma?"

Subhuti said to the Buddha, "World-honored One, the Tathagata has not said anything."

"Subhuti, what do you think? Is all the fine dust throughout the three thousand-fold world system a lot of dust or not?"

Subhuti said, "It is a lot, World-honored One."

"Subhuti, the Tathagata says that all of that fine dust is not fine dust, and that that is what is called fine dust. The Tathagata says that the world is not the world, and that is what is called the world."

As mentioned in the above passage from the *Diamond Sutra*, the Buddha uses the expression "three thousand-fold world system," which is a concept in Buddhist cosmology that refers to the entirety of the universe. The Buddha uses the example of the three thousand-fold world system being composed of so many particles of dust to show that neither the dust, nor the amalgamation of dust, are anything but illusory phenomena. They lack any intrinsic nature, and are merely a combination of causes and conditions. The Buddha speaks of *prajnaparamita,* so that living beings can realize the error of their ways and free themselves from suffering and obtain happiness. This is why the Buddha uses labels like "dust" and "world system" in the first place, so that he can employ skillful means to teach the Dharma to living beings at the right moment. All the worldly names and terms are used to skillfully lead people and communicate. With this in mind we should not abide in such names, for as soon as we become attached to them we can fall into the trap of delusion.

All things exist as a temporary combination of causes and conditions. All of our names and labels are temporary, as are all the sensations and experiences of the body and mind. People who practice meditation use expressions like "understand the mind and see intrinsic nature," "give rise to a mind that does not abide in anything," and "go directly to the inherent mind," but these are all describing the same thing: the inherent mind. The *Suramgama Sutra* describes the inherent mind as "always abiding in the true mind, the naturally pure and bright essence." The inherent mind has many other names as well: it is called the mind that always abides in truth, the bright mind, and the mind free from defilements. It is called naturally pure and essentially bright. It goes by the name *prajna* and *tathagatagarbha,*[1] and is described as a pure,

---

1. Sanskrit term meaning "womb of the Buddha," indicating where Buddhahood is born. Synonymous with Buddha nature. *Ed.*

bright light, but we can only see this pure, bright light when we are free of defilements. To "understand the mind and see intrinsic nature" means to understand one's inherent *prajna*, the *tahtaga-tagarbha*. This is precisely the meaning of the Buddhist verse by Sixth Patriarch Huineng:

> Essentially, bodhi is not a tree.
> The bright mirror is also not standing;
> Inherently, there is no thing,
> Where can it attract dust?

One day Bailing encountered Pang Yun on the road. Bailing asked, "Have you ever told anyone about the one verse you learned at Mazu Daoyi's place?"

Pang Yun said, "Sure, I have told it to someone."

Bailing did not understand. The one verse in question could not be told with language, nor could it be conceived of through thinking. No explanation of it would be right. So he asked Pang Yun again, "Who did you tell it to?"

Pang Yun pointed to himself and said, "I only told it to myself!"

Bailing said admiringly, "Even the Buddha's great disciple Subhuti, the foremost in understanding emptiness, would be no match for you."

In pointing at himself, Pang Yun was saying that the "one verse" was his own Buddha nature, of which everyone is endowed. Experiencing it is an internal affair, as in how one can know if some water is warm or cool only by drinking it. A direct experience cannot be communicated to others.

Pang Yun then asked Bailing, "Who have you told your one verse to?"

Bailing then put on his hat and left.

While it is true that the true reality of Buddha nature cannot be communicated in words, if one does not make use of the skillful means of spoken and written language, living beings will never learn the errors of their ways. That is why the Buddha joined the symbol of the diamond with the wondrous teachings on *prajna*. This symbol and the teachings share the same essence. They remove the afflictions that obscure the mind's vision, and point to our intrinsic nature, allowing us to attain *paramita* and "cross over." This is why the complete, Sanskrit title of the sutra is the *Vajra Prajnaparamita Sutra*.

All Phenomena Are Empty

 "The Dharma of which the Tathagata speaks cannot be held on to, it cannot be spoken, it is not a phenomenon, and it is not a non-phenomenon."

The word "phenomena" used above is a translation of the Chinese word *fa* (法). There are many ways to translate *fa*, but in this instance it means some element that enables us to understand things. Phenomena are the standards by which we can relate to each other and come to understand the principles of reality. In a Buddhist context, the term can be used to describe the names we give all things, and even concepts and ideas within the mind. "Phenomena" can express both the tangible and intangible. For example, we give names to phenomena like "flower," "house," "table," and so on so that we can talk about them and be comprehensible to others.

There is a verse which expresses the Buddhist understanding of "phenomena" well:

Phenomena are non-phenomena:
Open a fist and it's the palm of the hand once
    more;
Floating clouds drift across the azure sky:
For ten thousand miles it's all the same.

Consider a closed fist. If we were to call a fist a phenomenon, it is but an "unfixed phenomenon," for if someone with a closed fist opens his hand it becomes an open palm. All phenomena are like this: they can be good or bad, wholesome or unwholesome. They are not fixed or standardized. Considering the example of a fist again: if we hit someone with the fist, we see the fist as something "bad." But if a fist is used to massage someone's back and give them pleasure, then the fist is a good thing. This is why all phenomena are "unfixed phenomena." This is what the Buddha means when he says in the *Diamond Sutra* that phenomena cannot be held on to, for they are neither phenomena nor non-phenomena. Even the teaching of *prajna* cannot be considered wholesome, nor can it be considered unwholesome, for it is a truth that transcends the distinction of wholesome or unwholesome.

In Buddhism there is a bodhisattva named Avalokitesvara, who has a reputation for being able to liberate living beings far and wide. In fact, in the daily Chinese liturgy there is a chant about Avalokitesvara Bodhisattva:

The thirty-two manifestations respond to calls in
    all the numerous worlds;
Teaching and liberating Jambudvipa over a bil-
    lion *kalpas.*

"Jambudvipa" is a name for our universe in Indian cosmology, and the expression "billion *kalpas*" is an Indic reckoning of an immensely long period of time. The "thirty-two manifestations" is a reference to the thirty-two different forms of Avalokitesvara Bodhisattva described in the Universal Gate chapter of the *Lotus Sutra*. The sutra lists these thirty-two manifestations to show that Avalokitesvara Bodhisattva has the ability to adapt to the needs of the various kinds of living beings, with their differing capacities, to teach the Dharma to them. The thirty-two manifestations listed are: a Buddha, a *pratyekabuddha*, a *sravaka*, King Brahma, Lord Sakra, Isvara, Mahesvara, a great heavenly general, Vaisravara, a lesser king, an elder, a layperson, a minister, a Brahmin, a *bhiksu*, a *bhiksuni*, an *upasaka*, an *upasika*, a female elder, a female layperson, a female minister, a young boy or girl, a *deva*, a *naga*, a *yaksha*, a *gandharva*, an *asura*, a *garuda,* a *kimnara*, a *mahoraga*, and a *vajrapani*.[2]

Which one of these thirty-two manifestations is the true Avalokitesvara Bodhisattva? Each one of these thirty-two manifestations shows the bodhisattva employing skillful means to bring liberation to living beings. The Dharma cannot be held on to, nor can it be spoken. The Dharma as expressed in language is nothing more than the Buddha and Avalokitesvara Bodhisattva teaching the Dharma through skillful means in order to liberate living beings. Words like "*prajna*," "*paramita*," and "*vajra*," are all given so that living beings can attain enlightenment and live a life that is carefree.

Recall the metaphor of the three birds in the sky mentioned previously: a little sparrow might flap its wings with all its might,

2. The manifestations are specific Buddhist deities or classes of heavenly beings. For more information on some of these manifestations, see the glossary. *Ed.*

but it can only fly a distance of two or three yards. A pigeon on the other hand can flap its wings and vault over the tops of trees three to five yards tall. Yet an eagle can spread its wings and fly high into the blue sky.

Likewise, if a rabbit is trying to cross a river it has to frantically paddle with its little feet and will be fearful while crossing. A horse can cross a river paddling and swimming with its four feet with some difficulty. An elephant, however, will likely be able to reach the bottom of the river, and can cross the river with a relaxed gait until it reaches the other shore.

The sky is the same, though the three birds fly through it differently. The river is the same, though the three animals cross it differently. In the same way, the essence of human hardship is the same, though different people experience different levels of trouble in their life. If we can accomplish what is difficult to do and bear what is difficult to bear, then we will come to thoroughly realize the emptiness of *prajna*. It is only then that we can gradually come to cross the river of life to enlightenment like an elephant does: relaxed and at ease.

One day the Buddha was outside the gate to the Jeta Grove Monastery when he saw Ksudrapanthaka, one of his disciples, weeping and wailing. The Buddha asked, "Why are you standing here so sad and heartbroken?"

"Lord Buddha, my older brother finally got fed up with my stupidity. Because I can't seem to learn or memorize any of the teachings, he has driven me away and demanded that I return to lay life and go home. That is why I was crying."

The Buddha comforted him, and took him back to the monastery. The Buddha then handed Ksudrapanthaka a broom and told him to repeat the word "broom" again and again as he cleaned the monastery. Ksudrapanthaka felt grateful that not only did the Buddha take him in but also was kind enough to give him personal instruction. Afterwards, Ksudrapanthaka spent every day concentrating on the Buddha's instructions, and even though he was a slow learner, he was finally able to learn and memorize "broom" within a month's time.

Ksudrapanthaka concentrated on reciting "broom" with complete dedication, when one day he thought, "What is a broom? Something that sweeps and cleans the dirt and dust on the ground. So as I clean the monastery with the broom, I sweep and clean."

A few more days passed and Ksudrapanthaka began to think, "My body and mind have dust and grime, too. My afflictions are like dust and grime, while wisdom is like this broom which can sweep them clean."

This was how Ksudrapanthaka attained liberation and became an arhat.

The word "broom" is not a sacred foundation of the Dharma, so how was it able to bring someone to enlightenment and wisdom? The *Diamond Sutra* says:

 That which is called the Buddhadharma is not the Buddhadharma.

Saying the word "broom" aloud is not the Dharma, but when the mind deeply contemplates something it does not hold only what is or is not the Dharma, but instead simply aligns itself with the principles of Buddhism.

Let Go, Transcend, Abide in Nothing

What is real freedom? To find the answer, we must examine the mind, which is so prone to restlessness and distraction. When faced with impermanence, can the mind adapt to whatever circumstance without troubling you or annoying others? When faced with disputes, can the mind remain calm and composed and let things happen naturally? When faced with fame and fortune, can the mind transcend them serenely without getting caught up and imprisoned? When faced with separation, in life or in death, can the mind maintain right mindfulness and clarity? As long as we are able to handle the mind, we can live carefree without abiding in anything and be people who are truly virtuous and free.

Jinbifeng was an enlightened Chan master who had let go of desiring anything, save for a jade bowl that never left his side. Each time he sat down to meditate, he would first make sure to put his jade bowl away in a safe place. Only after he was sure it was safe could he meditate.

Then one day Yama, the lord of death, sent a few of his demons after Jinbifeng because his life had run out and he was fated to die. But because Jinbifeng was in a deep meditative state the demons were unable to seize his spirit. After a few days, the demons became quite worried, for they dared not return to Yama without Jinbifeng in tow.

Finally the demons went to petition a local earth deity and to ask him how they could get Jinbifeng to leave his meditative state. The earth deity gave them the following advice: "Jinbifeng is enlightened and has already let go of many of this world's attachments, but he still loves his jade bowl. Perhaps if you were to tamper with his jade bowl, a thought of the bowl would arise in his mind and he would leave his meditative state."

The little demons did as the earth deity had instructed: they found Jinbifeng's jade bowl and mischievously gave it a nudge. Sensing the bowl was not safe, Jinbifeng quickly emerged from his meditation and snatched the bowl away.

Now that Jinbifeng's spirit was before them, the demons clapped their hands and laughed, "Come along now, you're coming with us to see the lord of death!"

Jinbifeng realized that this single thought of desire was about to end his life, so he immediately smashed the jade bowl and returned to his meditative state. Within the emptiness of his meditation echoed the following verse:

> If you wish to seize Jinbifeng,
> Then you must lock up space with iron chains;
> And if empty space can indeed be locked up,
> Then you can come again and seize Jinbifeng.

Everyone has some kind of "jade bowl" within their heart: something they are unwilling to let go of. The "jade bowl" could be wealth, fame, love, power, or any of a variety of other things. If we are unwilling to smash the jade bowl that shackles our thoughts, then how are we to live without abiding in anything? No matter what it is that we become attached to, the mind can become affixed to it, making it impossible for us to realize what is truly most important in life. We can be free only when we let go of and transcend our attachments.

True Emptiness and Wondrous Existence

The Chan master Nan'in lived during Japan's Meiji era. In Japan, Chan is known as Zen, and one day a research professor came to Nan'in to ask about Zen. Nan'in received him and offered him a cup of tea.

Chan Master Nan'in poured tea into his guest's cup until it was full, and then continued to pour. The professor watched as the tea spilled out all over the table. After a moment, the professor spoke up:

"Master, the cup is already full and the tea is spilling out. You don't need to pour any more!"

"You are just like this cup, for inside you are full of your own views. You must first empty your mind of attachments before it is possible for our Zen tea to flow into your mind."

In Buddhist circles we commonly hear expressions like "empty the self" or "eliminate the self," but the true emptiness of the Dharma is not staring mindlessly into space or giving up in a negative way. Rather, it means not having "a notion of self, a notion of others, a notion of sentient beings, or a notion of longevity." To not possess these notions does not mean that we must abandon the notions of self, others, sentient beings, and longevity, but rather that we simply do not cling to the notion of self, the notion of others, the notion of sentient beings, and the notion of longevity. Even though we abide within notions, we should learn to turn away from them.

There is an old Buddhist verse that says, "True emptiness does not interfere with wondrous existence, for there cannot be wondrous existence without true emptiness." Emptiness is quite difficult to understand, for it is a truth not easily mastered. What exactly then does "emptiness" mean?

For most people there is a clear distinction between "emptiness" and "existence." Such people might think that anything that exists can't possibly be "empty," and anything that is empty can't possibly exist. But this is not emptiness as it is described in the *Diamond Sutra*. The emptiness of the *Diamond Sutra* is not absolute nothingness, but rather is something that can contain both existence and non-existence.

Consider again the metaphor of the fist: When one's fingers are clenched, the fist is clearly there. But when the five fingers are spread out, where did the fist go? The fist that was so clearly apparent has now disappeared. And if one were to say there is no fist, simply clenching one's fingers together and the fist appears once more. The *Diamond Sutra* uses its discussion of emptiness to show that nothing in the world remains constant and unchanging. There is nothing that exists independent of cause and effect. Existence is thus non-existence, and non-existence is also existence.

The idea that emptiness can contain both existence and non-existence is the very meaning of causes and conditions. What then are causes and conditions? Consider two people meeting: When two people meet and then separate, it is only after such a separation that they may meet again. The causal relationship between two people involves meeting, as well as separation. Where there was once flat ground, depending upon many causal factors, we can build a lofty skyscraper. But eventually, as we saw with the Twin Towers in New York, even a tall skyscraper can be made to fall to the ground. A skyscraper contains emptiness both in its construction and its collapse.

A plant slowly grows from a seed until it can sprout flowers, and then after those flowers bloom they will later fall to the ground, and become part of the soil that will allow other seeds to grow. After the flowers fall away, the plant may produce fruit, which becomes food for animals, or it may fall to the ground and rot. In this way the plant's seeds are spread around to begin new life. "Existence" and "non-existence" are points on the same circle where the starting point is also the ending point. By allowing the presence of both existence and non-existence, emptiness is the essence of the universe and the foundation of human life.

Buddhists commonly use the phrase "Amitofo," which is nominally the name of Amitabha Buddha, but actually encompasses many, many meanings. For example, when Buddhists first see each other, they may say "Amitofo," as a greeting, and then it means "Ah, you are here." When we see each other for the first time, "Amitofo" can be our "good morning." Before we are about to leave some place, we might say "Amitofo," and then it becomes "goodbye." If we see someone fall and hurt themselves, we may say "Amitofo," and then it becomes a way to express our caring for others. If we see a mother strike her child, we may say, "Ouch, Amitofo," as a way to express our sympathy and sadness. If we receive a gift, we may say "Amitofo" to express our gratitude.

"Amitofo" indeed can have many meanings, and it takes on each of these meanings depending upon the context of the conversation. Emptiness is just like "Amitofo" in that it is free of temporal, spatial, and contextual restrictions. It is merely a temporary label used for convenience to establish and communicate the Dharma.

Some people become afraid when talking about emptiness: If the sky, the earth, and everything in the world is empty, with even all our sons and daughters being empty, isn't this terrible? If everything is empty, doesn't that mean that we have nothing at all?

But that is not the case. The way that emptiness works is not too different from being a Buddhist monastic. A Buddhist monastic has left home to join the monastic order, but in doing so, everywhere can now be his home. Likewise we should not be afraid of not having any children, for as long as you possess the heart of a mother or father, then all the people in the world will be your children. We need not be afraid of living with no wealth, for as long as we can make a spiritual commitment, everything in the world is ours.

Remember Chan Master Nan'in: before inquiring about Zen, he wanted the professor to empty his mind of attachments. Only an empty briefcase can be packed with things, only an empty railroad car can carry passengers, only empty nostrils can breathe air, and only an empty mouth can eat food. Only when there is enough space can people live and move about.

The *Diamond Sutra* shows us how to live peaceably within emptiness, showing us how to live within the wondrous existence of true emptiness without clinging to the rise and fall of causes and conditions. We cannot enjoy this freedom until we no longer abide anywhere.

The Mind That Does Not Abide

In 1949, amidst the turmoil of the Chinese civil war, I joined many others who hastily left Mainland China for Taiwan, bringing nothing with me at all. After arriving in Taiwan, I wore a pair of wooden sandals for two years until the soles were worn through to the ground, and I only had one shirt that I wore for two or three years. I didn't even have a piece of paper or a pen to write with. There were people who felt sorry for me, but I did not feel lonely or destitute at all.

During that time, in my heart I felt a sense of fulfillment and abundance. The world was there for me as I roamed between heaven and earth, and all living beings were my friends. If I had felt any sense of hardship and saw myself as destitute, I would have felt sorry for myself; how then could I have stayed firm to the Buddhist life?

How could I feel fulfillment and happiness, even though I was faced with difficult circumstances? I owe it to the Dharma and the emptiness of *prajna*. They were why I could consider the benefits of being a monastic extraordinary and special. Everything that I am is a result of the Dharma's nurturing influence. Because of it I could feel one with the earth, its mountains and rivers, and feel a connection with all Buddhas and bodhisattvas.

Within the emptiness of *prajna*, I could have the entirety of the universe. None of us is ever truly alone or destitute. Material things and our relationships with others will come and go, but for life to be truly fulfilling, we need spiritual fulfillment, the kind of fulfillment that lies within. This is neither something that money can buy, nor is it something that anyone else can create for us on our behalf. We must rely on ourselves to understand the Dharma and the emptiness of *prajna*, and then we must confirm that understanding by practicing it in our own lives.

The diamond-like mind—firm and solid—is the emptiness of *prajna* and the inherent mind of enlightenment. In order to generate the aspiration for enlightenment and see that aspiration through in the real world means understanding the four key insights of the *Diamond Sutra*: giving without notions, liberating with no notion of self, living without abiding, and cultivation without attainment. Understanding these are the key lessons of the entire *Diamond Sutra*.

IV

Giving

Without Notions

On one occasion the Buddha and Ananda had entered the city to gather alms and they saw a group of children playing beside the street. The children were playing make believe, building homes and storehouses out of piles of sand that they had gathered. They were also pretending the sand was rice, which they stored in their sandy storehouses. One of the children saw the Buddha and innocently held up some of his sand-rice with his cupped hands and offered it to the Buddha. The Buddha received it with a smile.

Ananda was quite perplexed—why would the Buddha accept this pile of sand? Once they had returned from their alms round, Ananda joined his palms together and asked respectfully, "Lord Buddha, what merit can there be in that child's gift of sand? Why did you accept it?"

"Have you forgotten, Ananda? The Buddha never considers the beauty or value of a gift, but instead cares about the sincerity of the act. That child had a mind that was undefiled and free of discrimination, and because of this he was able to perform a supreme act of giving. It should not be treated with scorn. As for the child's merit in offering the sand, one hundred years after my *nirvana*, the child will be born as the king of a great country, and his name will be 'Asoka.'[1] The other children playing with him will all become his ministers and will support his rule. That child will make the Triple Gem of Buddha, Dharma, and Sangha flourish in the human world and he will build 84,000 reliquary stupas. This will enable those who already believe to increase their roots of goodness, while those who do not yet believe will have the opportunity to attain liberation."

The *Treatise on the Perfection of Great Wisdom* mentions three kinds of giving. The first is the giving of wealth and property, with the other two being giving fearlessness, and giving the Dharma. A description of each of the three is provided below:

1. Giving Wealth
   We give wealth so that we can relieve the suffering of those who are poor or sick and ensure their survival.

2. Giving Fearlessness
   If we uphold the precepts and cultivate patience and harmlessness, we will not seek revenge upon any foe or enemy. Such a person treats all life with loving-kindness, so that there is no need for fear or trepidation. When we have such limitless compassion, we can remove the fears of others, even if it puts a risk to our own personal safety, allowing living beings to develop faith in the Dharma.

---

1. Asoka the Great (304-232 BCE) was a Buddhist monarch of the Mauryan Empire, and the first to unite the region we now know as India. Asoka sponsored many Buddhist missions to other countries, and is largely responsible for Buddhism spreading throughout Asia. He is considered a model for Buddhist kingship. *Ed.*

3. Giving the Dharma
    By teaching the true Dharma, we can bring others to cultivate what is wholesome and get rid of what is unwholesome, and allow living beings to attain enlightenment and realize their self nature. Diligence will allow us to tirelessly persist in pursuing what is wholesome, meditative concentration will allow us to know the minds of living beings like a bright mirror or still waters, and our wisdom will help us to smoothly handle affairs and teach the Dharma correctly.

The *Diamond Sutra* teaches that we should "give without notions," which includes the three kinds of giving mentioned above, but extends and transcends them. The relevant passage is quoted below:

"Moreover, Subhuti, within this phenomenal world, a bodhisattva should practice giving without abiding in anything. This means that he should not give abiding in form, nor should he give abiding in sound, smell, taste, touch, or dharmas. Subhuti, a bodhisattva should not give abiding in any notion whatsoever. And why is this? If a bodhisattva gives without abiding in any notion whatsoever, then his merit will be immeasurable."

"Subhuti, what do you think, can the vastness of space to the east be measured?"

"No, it cannot, World-honored One."

"Subhuti, can the vastness of space to the south, west, north, up, or down be measured?"

"No, it cannot, World-honored One."

> "Subhuti, when a bodhisattva gives without abiding in any notion, his merit is just as immeasurable. Subhuti, a bodhisattva should abide in this teaching and this teaching alone."

The *Diamond Sutra* makes extensive use of the phrase *wuxiang bushi* (無相布施), "give without notions." This concept has wide-ranging meaning, but can be summarized by saying we should give and receive as the Buddha did in the opening story: without any notions or concepts based in phenomena, ideas, or outward appearances with which to discriminate or diminish ourselves as givers, who we give to, or what we give. There should be no clinging to the notions of self, others, sentient beings, or longevity, nor should one cling to the six sense objects of sights, sounds, smells, tastes, touch, and dharmas. The merit of giving without notions is limitless.

All Worldly Affairs Are Transient

Once upon a time there was a princess who was the favorite child of the king, and she was by his side from morning till night. One day it rained, and as the raindrops hit against the earth, bubbles began to appear. The princess saw the bubbles and was quite delighted with them. She said to her father, the king, "I want those bubbles made into a garland I can wear on my head."

The king said, "But these bubbles cannot even be grasped in our hands, how can they be made into a garland?"

Upset, the princess said, "If I don't get a garland made of bubbles, then I'll starve myself to death!"

The king then summoned his most skilled craftsmen and said to them, "You are all skilled craftsmen, and there is nothing that you cannot make. I command you to make me a garland of bubbles for my princess this instant. If you fail, I will have you all executed!"

The craftsmen were terrified. One of the craftsmen finally spoke up, "But making a garland out of bubbles is impossible!"

Just as the king was about to have them all executed, an elderly craftsman stepped forward and said to the king, "I can make a bubble garland for the princess."

The old craftsman then approached the princess and said, "The only problem is, I don't know which bubbles you like and which ones you don't. I beg you, your highness, please bring me your favorite bubbles, and then I will make the garland for you."

The princess agreed. But, as soon as she reached out to touch a bubble, it would pop. Even after working at it for a whole day she couldn't catch one single bubble. Then the princess realized that bubbles are like an illusion, made from the coming together of causes and conditions. As the *Diamond Sutra* says:

32

All conditioned phenomena
Are like dreams, illusions, bubbles, and shadows,
Like dew and lightning.
One should contemplate them in this way.

As we learned from the story of the princess and the above verse from the *Diamond Sutra*, phenomena are transitory. As identified in the verse, we should contemplate phenomena in six ways:

1. Contemplate Phenomena as Dreams
    Worldly phenomena are like dreams, for everything will pass away. Just as when waking from a dream,

once phenomena have dissipated they leave not the
slightest trace behind.

2. Contemplate Phenomena as Illusions
    Conditioned phenomena are illusory manifestations;
    they are not real. The effects of karma and the cycle
    of birth and death are manifestations as well. They
    are like a play performed on a stage: parents, siblings,
    friends, relatives, spouses and children all make an ap-
    pearance, yet the instant the curtain falls nothing is as
    it was. In a way, life is not truly life and death is not
    truly death.

3. Contemplate Phenomena as Bubbles
    Our emotions are like bubbles in that they are not
    long-lasting. Our joy, anger, sadness, and happiness,
    as well as the moments in between that are neither
    pleasure nor pain, are all as momentary and transient
    as bubbles.

4. Contemplate Phenomena as Shadows
    Worldly phenomena and all the experiences of human
    life are like shadows, in that they are not real.

5. Contemplate Phenomena as Dew
    The dew quickly disappears as soon as the sun comes
    out. Our bodies are not so different. For example, a
    baby is born and slowly grows into what we call a
    little girl; some more time passes and she becomes a
    female student, a young woman, and then later a wife,

a mother, and an old woman. Sickness and senility slowly make it impossible for her to live on her own, just like a little baby. Don't we often hear talk of a second childhood? Life changes bit by bit just like the morning dew.

6. Contemplate Phenomena as Lightning
Lightning is fleeting, there for just an instant, like time itself. The past, present, and future pass away quite quickly. Human life is also like lightning, for life exists in that short moment of breathing in and out. Once the breath stops, life is no more.

Once there was a theatre troupe based in a city that was experiencing a famine, so they decided to pack up their things and become a traveling theatre troupe, seeking opportunities in neighboring villages. When traveling to the next village they hurried as fast as they could, but they arrived so late that they were unable to find lodgings for the night and had to spend the night in the mountains. The temperatures ran low in the mountains that night, and it was bone-chillingly cold, so the troupe started a fire and slept beside it to stay warm.

One member of the troupe was sick and could not withstand the bitter cold, so he dug through their costume trunk and threw on the first thing he found for some extra warmth. What the actor failed to realize was that the costume he picked just happened to be the demon costume they used in their play. So there he sat, warmed in the glow of the fire and dressed as a fearsome demon.

In the middle of the night, another member of the troupe was awakened from a dream and saw the demon sitting by the fire. He remembered that he had heard stories that there were man-eating demons in the mountains, so he leapt to his feet and began yelling to wake the others. The commotion startled everyone, and they all began running for their lives in blind terror.

The actor wearing the demon costume saw how everyone was running and thought something bad must have happened, so he took flight in a desperate attempt to catch up to his friends. The people in front saw that the demon was running after them and became even more terrified. They began a mad rush forward, fearing for their lives, heedless of all the brambles, rocks, creeks, and gullies that lay in their path. Not until daybreak did they discover that the person chasing after them was not a demon at all, but actually one of their fellow actors. In the end they were exhausted and worn out, covered with cuts and bruises all over their bodies.

The *Diamond Sutra* says that all phenomena are like dreams, illusions, bubbles, shadows, dew, and lightning. We should not cling to such negative fantasies. Just as we cannot hold on to dew and lightning vanishes in an instant, the Buddha implores us to not abide in phenomena. Metaphors like this help to facilitate teaching the Dharma and show the impermanence of worldly things, reminding us not to cling to what is unreal amid all the phenomena that are presented to us so superficially. Instead we should strive to comprehend the essential nature of emptiness. As mentioned previously, "emptiness" encompasses both existence and non-existence, for it is cause and effect itself. We should learn to use what is illusory to pursue what is true, so that we can find the true reality of *prajna.*

Once there were two demons who were preparing to reincarnate into the world of the living. King Yama, the lord of death, spoke to them: "You two are going to be born as human beings. You can choose to be born in a life in which you always give things to other people, or you can choose to be born in a life in which you always receive things from other people. Into which life do you choose to be born?"

One of the demons knelt down and said, "King Yama, your majesty, I would like to be born as one who spends his life receiving things from others."

The other demon kept quiet, waiting to hear King Yama's plans.

With a rap of his gavel, King Yama announced his judgment:

"I decree that you be born in the human world as a beggar who must ask for things from others everywhere he goes."

"As for you," King Yama said, pointing at the second demon, "I decree that you shall be born into a rich and affluent family that regularly donates to charity."

The two demons were stunned and didn't know what to say.

Life is a journey, and when that journey has come to an end, we have the opportunity to look back upon the journey and understand its meaning and purpose. When we examine life in this way, we all learn one important lesson: things like chasing after material things, striving for real or empty glory, fighting to attain positions of power, building relationships, and other such things were only means by which we tried to maintain our lives, realize our ideals, and find meaning in life. But just as the *Diamond Sutra* says, they, too, are "like dreams, illusions, bubbles, and shadows. Like dew and lightning." Only when we look at life from the perspective that all things will end can we be diligent and shoulder life's responsibilities.

Food items each have a shelf life, and we must eat them before they go bad. Life is not so different. Life's journey will come to an end in due course, so we must cherish whatever happens along the way. Our lives are limited, and time will pass, so we must not simply go through the motions frittering our lives away. When our own journeys are reaching the end, if we look back and see how we spent our lives trying to get something out of people or taking advantage of others, we cannot help but feel regret.

Giving is the only way to be a truly wealthy person; for if the mind craves possessing and acquiring, then no matter how much wealth you have, you will still be as poor as a beggar.

With and Without Notions

The *Diamond Sutra* commonly uses the two character expression *bushi* (布施) to refer to giving. The character *bu* means "universal," while *shi* means "to scatter or disperse," designating an especially inclusive type of giving. Giving, in all of its many forms, is what allows us to disperse our gifts universally and eliminate our habitual illusory thinking and afflictions. Why then did the Buddha use the empty vastness of space as a metaphor for merit?

Whenever Chan Master Seisetsu Shucho gave Dharma talks at Engaku Temple many, many people would come. Whenever there was a talk the crowd would be so tightly packed into the hall that you could barely move. Finally, someone suggested that a new wing be added to the temple to allow for a more spacious lecture hall.

One devotee filled a bag with one hundred taels of gold and brought it to the temple to give to Chan Master Seisetsu, explaining that the donation was to fund the building of the lecture hall. Seisetsu received the gold and then quickly busied himself with other matters.

The devotee was extremely displeased by the Chan master's attitude. He thought to himself, "One hundred taels of gold is no small amount of money. How could the master receive such a large donation and not bother saying a single word of thanks?"

So the devotee followed Seisetsu and dropped a little hint, "Master, you know there are one hundred taels of gold in that bag I gave you."

Seisetsu responded coolly, "You already told me. I'm aware."

The devotee raised his voice, "Hey! I donated one hundred taels of gold today!"

Seisetus had just reached the main shrine, and stopped.

"If you would like to treat donating money to the Buddhas like some sort of business deal, then on behalf of the Buddhas I can offer you a word of thanks for this transaction. Now consider the account between you and them settled."

This may be a Chan story, but it does remind us as well that we must not fixate on notions. In the *Diamond Sutra* the Buddha uses the vastness of space as a metaphor for the merit of giving. Since karmic effects are related to karmic causes, we should ensure that when we give, our minds are also as open and genuine as space. When there is no favoritism or partiality, the positive karmic effect is as vast and extraordinary as space itself. We must be able to look upon all living beings as if they were our own children in order to inwardly destroy any miserly attitudes and outwardly perform beneficial deeds. There are three contemplations we can practice to help us foster a mind of equality that can accept all living beings and be as broad and expansive as the vastness of space. They are:

1. Contemplation of Renunciation
   Contemplate the habitual karmic tendencies that carry on throughout the cycle of birth and death and the

suffering and pain they bring to the body and mind. Observe and think carefully about how the body is as fleeting as foam on water and life is short. By contemplating renunciation in this way, we will not cling greedily to external wealth and property and can perform great acts of giving.

2. Contemplation of Enlightenment
   Contemplate the dignified and magnificent physical features of the Buddha, and contemplate the pure morality that is the nature of the Dharma. By contemplating these you will come to see that there are no distinctions between one's own mind, the Buddha, and all living beings. One will realize that our original enlightened nature is universal, and this will allow one to perform acts of giving out of reverence for all living beings.

3. Contemplation of Compassion
   Consider all the negative karma that living beings create when they fail to encounter the Buddha, when they fail to understand the Dharma, and when they do not respect the monastic community because they do not know the Triple Gem and do not believe in cause and effect. Such a person is like a drunken man trying to walk down the street or a legless man trying to cross a river. You should care for living beings in the same way that you would care for your own body if it were covered with open wounds and dedicate all your attention to protecting and helping them.

Once there was a town in Taiwan hit by a particularly fearsome flash flood, such that people had to climb up to their roofs to avoid the rising water. One man trapped in the flood was an especially pious Buddhist, and as the floodwaters began to cover his feet, he began to urgently pray:

"O, Great Compassionate Avalokitesvara Bodhisattva, please come quickly and save me!"

Not long afterwards, a Taiwanese aborigine saw the praying man and rowed his canoe over to save him. As the canoe approached, the man shouted at the aborigine, "No, I don't want one of you mountain tribespeople coming to save me! I want the compassionate Avalokitesvara Bodhisattva to come and save me."

The storm waters continued to rise and climbed up to his waist. He prayed even more anxiously, "O, compassionate Avalokitesvara Bodhisattva, come quickly and save me!"

Then a speedboat zoomed by, offering to take him to safety, but again the praying man turned them down.

"I have detested science and technology all my life. I can't stand anything mechanical, no matter what it is. I want the compassionate Avalokitesvara Bodhisattva to come and save me!"

The flood waters had now already risen to his chest and he was yelling in alarm and fear, "Avalokitesvara Bodhisattva, come quickly and save me!"

Then there came an American flying a helicopter to save him, but the praying man waved the pilot off with his hands and said, "You're a foreigner! I don't want a foreigner saving me. I want Avalokitesvara Bodhisattva to save me!"

Just when he was about to drown, the praying man was saved by a Chan master. He said to the Chan master, "I've been pious and faithful, how come Avalokitesvara Bodhisattva did not come to save me?"

The Chan master replied, "You're really doing Avalokitesvara Bodhisattva an injustice. You called out for help and the bodhisattva tried to save you again and again. The bodhisattva manifested as a canoe, a speedboat, and a helicopter to come and save you. Not only were you ungrateful, but you were picky, as well."

Once greed, grasping, and attachment arise in our consciousness, we become like the blind men trying to learn what an elephant is by touching it;[2] it is impossible for us to perceive the whole of reality. Avalokitesvara Bodhisattva does not liberate living beings through any fixed method or employing any fixed appearance. In performing acts of giving in this world, we must do so without notions, for in that way merit can become limitless.

There are plenty of Buddhists who come to the temple to bring a few bananas and apples and donate a little money for incense and lamp oil in hope of seeking good fortune, honor, and power and asking for protection, wealth, and other benefits. This kind of giving abides and is invested in the six sense objects (sights, sounds, smells, tastes, touch, and dharmas). It is not too different from trying to bribe the gods or offering something with strings attached.

If the thought behind a gift is not pure then the gift has some notion behind it, and the merit to be gained from such a gift is limited. Examples of such notions are giving to obtain fame, rewards, or advantages, giving out of fear of being reborn in the lower realms of existence, or even giving for the sake of one's own

---

2. An allusion to a well-known parable in which a group of blind men encounter an elephant. Each feels a different part of the elephant, coming to a different conclusion about what an elephant is. For example, one touches the tail and thinks an elephant is like a rope, one touches the leg and thinks an elephant is like a pillar, etc. *Ed.*

health or fortune. But if something is given with no thought of reward or benefit, but is given only for the sake of living beings and meeting their needs, that is giving without notions. The merit from giving without notions is limitless.

 "For this reason, Subhuti, a bodhisattva should turn away from all notions, and initiate the mind of *anuttara samyaksambodhi.* He should not give rise to a mind abiding in form, and he should not give rise to a mind abiding in sound, smell, taste, touch, or dharmas. He should give rise to a mind that does not abide in anything. If the mind abides in anything it is a false abiding. Thus, the Buddha says that a bodhisattva should not give abiding in form. Subhuti, a bodhisattva should give in this way to benefit all sentient beings. The Tathagata says that all notions are not notions, and therefore he also says that all sentient beings are not sentient beings."

"Subhuti, the Tathagata is a speaker of what is true, what is real, what is so, what is not deceptive, and what is not altered. Subhuti, the Dharma that the Tathagata has attained is not real and it is not unreal."

"Subhuti, when the mind of a bodhisattva abides in phenomena and practices giving he is like a person who has entered into darkness—he sees nothing at all. When the mind of a bodhisattva does not abide in any phenomena and practices giving, he is like someone who has eyes in the full light of the sun—he sees all forms clearly."

Sixth Patriarch Huineng wrote in his *Exegesis on the Diamond Sutra*:

> When giving one should have a pure, undefiled mind. First, do not seek to dignify your own appearance. Second, do not seek the pleasures of the five desires.[3] Giving eliminates miserliness internally and benefits all living beings externally.

Giving without notions means that there is no "self" giving the gift, no "self" that receives the gift, and that the gift itself doesn't even have a "self." Naturally there is no thought of any sort of reward coming from the gift after it has been given either. Only when the essence of these three aspects is empty does it become "giving without notions," and the merit of such an act of giving becomes limitless.

As long as we maintain our compassion while we talk, work, eat, and dress during our everyday lives, we will be able to help others at every turn and bring benefit to the larger community. We must make sure not to weigh every gain or loss in our relationships, nor inhibit our giving with considering if we should give more or less.

When we give we should keep in mind four things:

1. Do not wish for some extraordinary circumstances, but give as conditions allow.
2. Do not be stingy, but give what you can.
3. Do not distinguish between beloved friends and hated foes, but give to both joyfully.
4. Do not be deluded by the idea of some future reward, but do so for the sake of giving.

---

3. Wealth, sex, fame, food and drink, and sleep. *Ed.*

As we cultivate the three karmas of body, speech, and mind, it is easiest to give through the karma of speech. It does not take a large amount of wealth or very much time to put in some good words. Good words are just like the smell of flowers, in that they infuse others with joy and happiness.

One day a brahman came storming into the Buddha's Bamboo Grove Monastery outside of the city of Rajagrha, looking for trouble. Many of the brahman's relatives had joined the monastic order, and this was something that infuriated the brahman to no end. So the brahman slandered and defamed the Buddha with his harsh words, claiming that the Buddha had bewitched his friends through black magic. The Buddha listened to the brahman's abusive tirade quietly, the Buddha spoke:

"Suppose you were visiting a friend and brought a gift, but your friend steadfastly refused to accept the gift that you brought, what would you do?"

The brahman answered, "If my friend truly refused to accept my gift, then the only thing I could do would be to take it back home."

The Buddha said, "I refuse to accept any of the language you tried to give to me today, so all those spiteful, abusive words are yours to keep."

Under no circumstances should we utter abusive words, use our language to make hell for other people, or fall into the hell of language created for us by others. If we can instead speak the Buddha's four kinds of right speech to anyone, anywhere, then we will naturally be able to dissolve the conflicts and misunderstandings that arise between people:

1. Speak good words that are pure and undefiled.
2. Speak wonderful words that put an end to dissension and conflict.
3. Speak true words that reflect the true Dharma and the right path.
4. Speak Dharma words that bring benefit, peace, and happiness.

A long time ago there were two geese living in the wild forest. The geese were good friends with a turtle who lived in a nearby pond. During one summer there was a long dry spell where there was no rain, and the water in the pond dried up. The turtle was getting anxious, if the drought continued there was no way he would be able to survive. The two geese felt sorry about the turtle's predicament, and they wanted to help him move to a new place with water. The two geese came up with an idea: They would use a tree branch and have the turtle hold the middle part in its mouth, then the two of them would each hold an end and they would be able to lift the turtle to a new location. The two geese advised the turtle that, as long as he kept his mouth shut and did not talk for any reason, they would be able to transport him to safety.

The two geese then flew high into the sky carrying the turtle. When they passed through the sky above a village, a group of children pointed at the sky and yelled, "Come and look everyone! Looks like these geese caught themselves a turtle!"

The turtle became annoyed with the children and thought he was being humiliated. Burning with rage, the turtle yelled at the children: "What do you know? These geese didn't catch me at all!"

The instant the turtle opened his mouth to yell at the children he fell out of the sky.

Giving Wealth

The purpose of the diamond-like wisdom of *prajna* is to allow us not to hold on to notions of phenomena or notions of non-phenomena. Thus we can know that the Buddha genuinely wishes us to attain enlightenment, and employs skillful means to teach us, just as when trying to cross a river we may borrow a small boat to reach the other side. The following *gongan* illustrates this point:

It was a bitterly cold day in winter and snow had already been falling for three days. On that day a beggar came knocking on Chan Master Myoan Eisai's door. The Chan master opened the door revealing the beggar, shivering in the cold, who said, "Chan master, my family and I have not had a grain of rice for many days now, and the heavy snowfall day after day has also caused my old illness to return. I beg you sir, please help us!"

But the monastery had no surplus food or money, so how could Eisai help them? Suddenly he remembered that they had some gold foil on hand for gilding the Buddha statue. And so without the slightest hesitation, he gave the gold foil to the beggar to meet his desperate need.

The Chan master's disciples were not very happy with him, and objected by saying, "Master, that gold foil was for gilding the Buddha statue. How could you give it away so carelessly?"

The Chan master answered calmly, "I only did so to pay homage to the Buddha."

One disciple countered, "Master, you took the gold foil intended for the sacred statue of the Buddha and gave it away. How can that be considered paying homage to the Buddha?"

Chan Master Eisai raised his voice to rebuke them, "The Buddha cultivated the Way for many *kalpas*, and did not care if he gave away his very blood, flesh, and marrow! How did the Buddha treat all living beings? You only see the gilded Buddha statue, but how do you not see the Buddha's heart?"

The *Diamond Sutra* teaches us that by giving without notions, we can be granted limitless merit. It also states that the gift of Dharma is superior to material gifts. It is easy to give material things once one's needs have been met, but making it possible for living beings to develop their own wisdom from within is not something that can be done by relying upon money and material goods alone. Even so, gifts of wealth and property can offer temporary help and survival to living beings. When the Buddha advises us to not give with notions, it does not mean that the Buddha is negating giving wealth altogether.

What steps can we take to ensure that when we give the kind of material support that is needed in our modern world that we do so without notions? For example, material support can be used to establish schools in remote and backward regions. By approaching projects like this, the material gifts can be used for more than just relieving the temporary needs of the body, like warmth and sustenance.

One day King Prasenajit had an audience with the Buddha and gave him the following report: "Lord Buddha, within the kingdom of Sravasti there is a certain elder named Mahanaman. He possesses vast treasuries of gold and silver, and millions of billions of precious stones such that it would be impossible to count them all. He also owns an unaccountably large number of houses and estates. Mahanaman possesses thousands of bushels of money and other valuables and tens of thousands of acres of farmland, yet he cannot find any enjoyment in all this wealth. Every day he eats coarse bran, rice crumbs, and other leftover and rotting food. He wears cheap and shoddy clothes and rides in a dilapidated, old cart. He has never made offerings to Buddhist monastics or brahman priests, nor has he ever given alms to poor and destitute beggars. Whenever he takes his meals, he is sure to lock the doors and windows tightly in fear that someone might come to his door and ask him for alms. Lord Buddha, the rich and affluent Mahanaman lives such an impoverished and fearful life. How should we use wealth in a way that is in accordance with the right path?"

The Buddha answered, "Great King, people like Mahanaman have minds that are crammed with ignorant and wicked ideas. Though they possess abundant material wealth, they cannot make use of it. They do not know about caring for their parents or supporting their family and relatives. They neither aid their slaves and servants nor share their wealth with their friends and comrades. They do not know that making offerings to Buddhist monastics or brahman priests is planting seeds in a field of merit to secure the blessings of happiness. Mahanaman does not understand how to broadly make use of his wealth to obtain worldly joy or transcendent merit."

"Great King, greedy, miserly people are like land with hard, alkaline soil. Though the land may have some pools of water, no one is willing to drink from them because of their bitter, salty taste. In the end, these pools will dry up and disappear. Generous people are like a country hamlet with a pure spring that produces good water. The pure water allows nearby trees to grow and prosper, and it engenders soft fragrant grasses and all kinds of fresh flowers and fruits. All living beings are able to bathe in its pool of water, and when tired and thirsty, they can partake of the pure spring waters and fine fruits. The animals of the forest can frolic about happily without fear. Great King, those who have wealth should be like the crystal-clear spring, for they use their wealth to make people happy and satisfied. Such people are carefree and affluent in this life, and will be reborn in the heavenly realms after death, where they will enjoy the blessings of happiness."

How long is a person's life, really? It passes as quickly as the morning dew, a bolt of lightning in the sky, froth upon the water, or a flickering flame. Our wealth is very limited, so how can we use it to fulfill our spiritual nature and continually build our lives around the principles of the wise, so that we can give without abiding in anything? I would recommend the following:

1. Organize around human feeling, not profits.
2. Organize around community, not individuals.
3. Organize around good friendship, not money.
4. Organize around contentment, not the five desires.

Material wealth will eventually be exhausted and turn to ruin one day, but not immaterial wealth. Such immaterial wealth as the relationships between people, the sharing of accomplishments, the guidance and care of good friends, the peace of hearing the Dharma, and others can enable us to organize ourselves around our internal wealth.

Giving Fearlessness

On May 15, 1992, a bus full of students, parents, and teachers from Jiankang Kindergarten in Taipei was going on a fieldtrip when the bus suffered an equipment failure and caught fire near the town of Taoyuan. Lin Jingjuan, one of the teachers at the kindergarten, could have escaped from the bus, but instead she rushed into the part of the bus that was engulfed in flames. Risking her life, she went to save the children from the raging fire and delivered them one by one to those helping by the side of the road, saving as many as she could. In the end, the body of Lin Jingjuan, blackened by the fire, was found in the wreckage of the bus, still holding tightly to the charred remains of a few children she was trying to protect.

Lin Jingjuan willingly suffered the pain of the flames and her scorched skin to save others. Amid the greatest suffering can be found humanity's greatest compassion. Lin Jingjuan was a tremendously brave individual who gave her life to others without the slightest trace of fear, a true bodhisattva. She calls to mind Avalokitesvara Bodhisattva, "the giver of fearlessness," who grants to all living beings that same sense of courageousness and fearlessness.

The merit to be gained from "filling the three thousand-fold world system with the seven treasures" as mentioned in the *Diamond Sutra* would surely be worthwhile, but giving material wealth is still limited and imperfect. Giving fearlessness provides the merit of great compassion, which is vastly superior to hundreds of years of good deeds expecting merit in return. Giving fearlessness is the application of true compassion. As mentioned earlier, the giving of fearlessness does not distinguish between beloved friends and hated foes, but seeks to free all living beings from fear and trepidation and allow them to establish faith in the Dharma. When people have a pure and persistent faith, they become able to apply wondrous *prajna* wisdom.

During the time of the Buddha, there lived a woman named Queen Mallika, who was the wife of King Prasenajit of Kausala and a very devout Buddhist. She followed and upheld the precepts and was well loved and respected by the common people. One day King Prasenajit wanted to have the royal cook killed over some trivial matter. When Queen Mallika heard the news, she was in the middle of an eight precept retreat,[4] but even so she dressed in fine clothing and invited her husband to enjoy an evening of food and wine with her, stipulating that the cooking was to be done by the very same cook.

King Prasenajit was quite perplexed, so he asked Queen Mallika, "You usually don't drink a drop of wine, and today you are observing the eight precepts. Why have you put on your jeweled necklaces and broken your fast to enjoy food and wine with me?"

Lady Mallika answered calmly, "I have heard that this royal cook has incurred your wrath, great king, and will soon be beheaded. If I do not ask him to prepare a delicious meal today, I am afraid I will never have another chance to do so."

The king then pardoned the royal cook.

Out of compassion, Lady Mallika acted in spite of the damage to her own reputation that the breaking of her vows would bring. Not only did she save the royal cook's life, but she also spared King Prasenajit from his momentary ignorance.

---

4. The eight precepts are an extension of the five precepts, and are often observed by lay practitioners on one-day short-term monastic retreats. In addition to the five precepts, they include not eating after noon, not wearing jewelry or sleeping in a high, luxurious bed, and an intensifying of the third precept to refrain completely from any sexual conduct. *Ed.*

Giving Dharma

"Subhuti, what do you think? If someone were to fill the three thousand-fold world system with the seven treasures, used them for giving, and attained merit for this, would the merit be great?"

Subhuti said, "It would be very great, World-honored One. And why is this? Such merit is not the nature of merit; thus the Tathagata says it is great."

"If someone else were to receive and uphold as few as four lines of verse from this sutra, and if he were to explain them to others, his merit would be even greater than that. And why is this? Subhuti, all Buddhas and all the supremely enlightened teachings of the Buddhas are born of this sutra."

In the above passage the Buddha says that the merit of someone who is able to faithfully receive and uphold the *Diamond Sutra,* even a mere four lines of verse from it, and explain them to others far exceeds that of a person who gives the seven treasures. Why?

Because even a gift as massive as filling the three thousand-fold world system with the seven treasures is a conditioned phenomenon. Since such a gift has limits, the merit of such a gift is limited. But giving the Dharma through teaching others is an unconditioned phenomenon. Offering teachings can help living beings eliminate their afflictions, end the cycle of birth and death, transcend the three realms, and attain Buddhahood. This is why the merit of giving the Dharma exceeds that of giving wealth.

The Buddha also says in the above passage that all Buddhas and all enlightened teachings are born out of the *Diamond Sutra.* The *Diamond Sutra's* teaching on "not abiding in anything" is derived from the larger teaching on emptiness as containing both existence and non-existence. This is *prajna,* which is also called "the mother of all Buddhas," and all living beings are endowed with intrinsic *prajna* nature.

 "Subhuti, suppose a person give a quantity of the seven treasures equal to all the Sumeru mountains within a three thousand-fold world system; if another person were to use this *Prajnaparamita Sutra,* even as few as four lines of verse, and receive, uphold, read, chant, and explain it to others, his merit would be one hundred times—nay, a hundred million, billion times, nay, an incalculable number of times that cannot even be suggested by metaphors—greater."

As the Buddha explains, no matter how many times one were to give the seven treasures, the merit and wisdom obtained does not equal even one hundred million billionth of that obtained through the giving of the Dharma. Indeed no numerical analogy can possibly quantify the difference, because giving the seven treasures is necessarily done so with certain notions. Whether a gift is as high as the mountains or as deep as the ocean, there will come a time when the mountain crumbles and the ocean dries up. In the same way, the merit and wisdom of such a gift will be exhausted. But one who receives and upholds the profound, notionless, *prajna* wisdom of the *Diamond Sutra* or explains it to others, even so little as four verses of the sutra, the merit and wisdom is immeasurably, incalculably large. It is infinite.

Once Manjusri Bodhisattva asked the Buddha, "What does it mean to 'give the seven treasures of the body'?"

The Buddha answered, "Such is the gift of non-desire. The eye without desire to see marvelous things is the gift of the sight treasure. The ear without desire to hear pleasant music is the gift of the sound treasure. The nose without desire to smell fine fragrances is the gift of the smell treasure. The tongue without desire to taste fine delicacies is the gift of the taste treasure. The body without desire for fine clothing is the gift of the touch treasures. The mind without desire for fame, fortune, or affection is the gift of the dharma treasure. Having no worldly desires is the gift of the Buddha treasure. If you can realize the gift of the seven treasures within your own body, the merit obtained will exceed the merit of giving the seven treasures of gold, silver, lapis lazuli, pearls, carnelian, coral, and amber. The merit of giving the seven treasures does not amount to one hundred million billionth of the former, even such a numerical analogy falls short."

Not having desire for something means not clinging or attaching to it, which is the same as "not abiding" in it. We cannot possibly exchange the seven treasures to obtain our intrinsic *prajna* nature. Our intrinsic *prajna* nature is extraordinarily precious. Only the pure, enlightened mind makes it possible to give the gift of the Dharma to others, so its merit will naturally exceed the giving of wealth.

⟨ 15 ⟩ "Subhuti, suppose a good man or good woman were to give as many of his or her lives as there are grains of sand in the Ganges River in the morning, and give as many of his or her lives as there are grains of sand in the

Ganges River at noon, and give as many of his or her lives as there are grains of sand in the Ganges River in the afternoon, and that this giving continued for infinite hundreds of millions of billions of kalpas; if someone were to hear this sutra, believe it, and not turn his mind against it, his merit would be greater—what of the merit of one who copies, receives, upholds, reads, chants, and explains it to others?"

"Subhuti, in summation, the virtue of this sutra is infinite and unlimited. The Tathagata speaks this sutra to those who have initiated the mind of the Great Vehicle; he speaks it to those who have initiated the mind of the Supreme Vehicle. For those who receive, uphold, read, chant, and explain this sutra to others, the Tathagata fully knows and fully sees that such people will attain infinite, immeasurable, limitless, inconceivable virtue. All such people will shoulder the *anuttara samyaksambodhi* of the Tathagata. And why is this? Subhuti, those who delight in the lesser Dharma cling to a view of self, a view of others, a view of sentient beings, and a view of longevity, and thus they are not able to listen to this sutra, to receive it, to read it, to chant it, or to explain it to others."

In the above passage from the *Diamond Sutra* the Buddha says that the merit of giving the Dharma even exceeds giving one's own life. If someone were to give his life as many times as there are grains of sand in the Ganges River three times a day for hundreds of millions of billions of *kalpas*, the merit gained from this would be impossible to calculate. Even so, if a person listens to the teachings of the *Diamond Sutra*, realizes the truth of *prajna,* and vows to practice according to its teachings and goes on to copy, receive and uphold, read, chant, and explain the *Diamond Sutra* to others, then the merit such a person would gain would exceed that of giving one's life so many times. However, if someone were to cling to a view of self, a view of others, a view of sentient beings, or a view of longevity, then they cannot possibly attain realization into *prajna* wisdom that is notionless and abides in nothing, nor can they possibly read and chant the sutra, much less explain it to others.

There are ten common practices for sharing the *Diamond Sutra* as a gift of Dharma with others. They are:

1. Copy and transcribe the sutra.
2. Make offerings of the sutra in a temple or Buddha hall.
3. Bestow the sutra on others by printing and circulating it.
4. Listen to the sutra and devote attention to learning its teachings.
5. Explain the sutra to others, removing their impediments to understanding the text.
6. Receive and uphold the teachings of the sutra and apply them in life to benefit oneself and others.
7. Teach the sutra by giving Dharma talks on the meaning of the sutra, enabling other to realize their intrinsic nature.
8. Chant mindfully and concentrate upon the sutra.
9. Contemplate the sutra, and silently plumb the depths of its ideas, and gain insight into its profound meaning.
10. Cultivate the sutra by thinking and pondering its profound meaning, practice its teachings extensively, and attain enlightenment.

The *Flower Adornment Sutra* states:

> Just as a gemstone in the dark
> Cannot be seen without a light;
> If no one preaches the Dharma,
> Even the wise cannot attain realization.

People who teach the Dharma are like bright lamps, for they are able to illuminate the subtleties of the Dharma for others. Without someone to teach the Dharma, there can be no attainment of enlightenment, no matter how intelligent living beings may be. This is a clear demonstration of the value of giving the Dharma.

Everyone Can Give

I have traveled all around teaching the Dharma, and have received expensive gifts of various kinds, but the one that touched me the most was a small yellow flower offered by a little girl in Ladakh on India's northern border.

As I was leaving Ladakh, my car began to move and part from the sea of well-wishers that had gathered to see me off, but I had already caught sight of a little girl holding a small yellow flower. She was shyly looking towards me, with the corners of her mouth pursed. She came dashing over just as the car was leaving, and stuck the yellow flower she held in her hand on the window. I hastened to tell the driver to stop, and took off the crystal prayer beads I wore on my wrist and gave them to her. She smiled sweetly, her eyes brimming with tears. Then the car began moving again, with the petals of the flower slightly quivering in the wind. I watched her in the car's rearview mirror, holding her pose with her palms joined in the distance. I was left feeling deeply touched for a long, long time. The purity that children have is the inherent *prajna* of their Buddha nature, which makes them all Buddhas to be.

Flowers only blossom for a time, each human life has an end, but the life of wisdom is infinite. People often think, "I'll wait until I have more money, and then I'll be able to give the seven treasures," or "I can't possibly give fearlessness until I can stand firmly in my own intrinsic nature," or "I'll wait until I am enlightened, and then I will give the Dharma." And yet at that moment that small yellow flower was the only thing the child had, and that was what she gave.

One who has not yet generated the aspiration for enlightenment is still an ordinary person, but once that aspiration has been made that person becomes a bodhisattva.

Do not be idle waiting for the right moment or look for other reasons and excuses not to give. Everybody can be giving, and be giving now. Give rise to the most treasured mind: that which gives without the slightest hesitation.

V

Liberation

With No Notion of Self

After Fifth Patriarch Hongren passed on the robe and alms bowl to Huineng, he knew that for awhile no one in the monastic community would understand why he suddenly made Huineng his successor, nor would they be able to accept him. So he had Huineng leave the monastery in the middle of the night. Hongren escorted Huineng to a dock at Jiujiang and offered to row Huineng across the river. As Hongren was manning the oars, Huineng said, "Venerable Master, please be seated. Your disciple should row."

Hongren replied by saying, "It is only fitting that I ferry you across."

In Chinese the word *du* (渡) means both "ferry" as well as "liberate." Hongren's words meant that, since he was Huineng's teacher, he saw it as his responsibility to be the one to "ferry" him to liberation.

Huineng replied, "When I was deluded, my teacher ferried me across. Upon awakening, I ferry myself."

わ ໑

What Huineng means by "ferrying himself" or "liberating himself" is that it is up to us to accumulate merit, make positive karmic connections, and cultivate wisdom. In Buddhism it is commonly said that we should "cultivate both merit and wisdom," as well as "emphasize both practice and understanding." This is precisely the process of self-liberation. Helping others is the root of happiness, and in accumulating merit we should serve others as we are inclined and as our circumstances allow. Examples include building bridges, paving roads, aiding in disaster relief, and assisting the poor.

To truly learn Buddhism, we must connect with others. Spiritual practice cannot be an excuse for selfishness or indolence, nor can it be an excuse to escape or distance oneself from the community. Our practice should create broad karmic connections that can help to build a positive future and to foster limitless merit and virtue. The meaning of a human life comes from the karmic seeds we are able to plant and witness them bear fruit in our field of merit before our lives come to an end.

We gain merit from joyfully giving out of kindness. During his many lifetimes of practice, the Buddha once cut off a piece of his own flesh to feed an eagle, and in another lifetime sacrificed his body to provide food for a tiger, as well as being born as the king of deer and the king of fish. The Buddha was able to broadly and universally give aid without distinguishing between friend or foe, self or other, whenever living beings were in need or facing difficulty. This did not happen on just one or two occasions, for the Buddha spent three great *kalpas* perfecting his virtue and wisdom such to become a Buddha, and one hundred small *kalpas* perfecting the major and minor physical characteristics of a Buddha.

If a person spends his entire life in this world only concerned with himself, with the "I," and working and toiling just to feed that one mouth and belly, that is a meaningless, wasted life. A person who does not understand *prajna* wisdom will desperately try to seek knowledge outside of himself, or he may parade around with his knowledge and abilities trying to show off how smart he is. Such a person may come to feel superior, like he is somehow more intelligent or handsome than most other people. The "I" appears to rise above the mass of common people to be in a class by itself. He becomes convinced that this "I" is not like all the others; it is the most beautiful lotus growing out of the mud. When someone thinks this way he has become attached to the notion of self.

Physically a human body is nothing more than a smelly bag of skin, something that has arisen from a combination of causes and conditions. All day long people only think about how they can dress themselves in fine clothes and eat good food, or how they can rise to some new and better position of power. But people who only live for themselves will find that, when their lives draw to a close and it's time to go, everything is merely a dream, an illusion, a bubble, or a shadow. It does not matter how they dressed themselves in elegant, name-brand finery, what positions of power they enjoyed, or how refined their meals were—it all vanishes into thin air.

Everybody has Buddha nature. It is just ignorance that makes one a sentient being and enlightenment that makes one a Buddha. And the difference between ignorance and enlightenment can lie in a single thought.

With all the hustle and bustle of human life, we should ensure that the mind and body have a place where they can find safety and security, and then allow others to find security as well. Some ways we can find security are:

1. Find security in the four immeasurables: loving-kindness, compassion, joy, and equanimity.
2. Find security by generating the aspiration for enlightenment and making a vow to liberate all living beings.
3. Find security in *prajna* wisdom.
4. Find security in meditative concentration and morality.
5. Find security in pure thoughts and reverence.
6. Find security in simplicity and humility.
7. Find security in letting go and being carefree.
8. Find security in learning and contentment.

Where Is the Self?

The *Diamond Sutra* says that we should have "no notion of self, no notion of others, no notion of sentient beings, and no notion of longevity."

Buddhism often speaks of the doctrine of "non-self," the lack of an inherent self-identity, and equates it with emptiness. "Non-self" means that all things arise from causes and conditions, and have no independent self-nature.

In order for something to rightly be called a "self," it must possess the following four conditions: autonomy, permanency, universality, and freedom. However, if the self is formed through causes and conditions related to the four great elements of earth, water, fire, and wind, it could not exist apart from them and is thus not autonomous. The self also exists only temporarily through the process of dependent origination, so it is not permanent. The self is obstructed everywhere, so it is not universal, and because the self is subject to the karmic effects of suffering, it is not free. The existence of the "self" is like a dream, an illusion, a bubble, a shadow, or like dew and lightning. It is merely a temporary self, formed by the combination of the five aggregates, which has no truly real nature. However, we must make use of this temporary self in order to find the true self of *prajna*.

By advocating "no notion of self, no notion of others, no notion of sentient beings, and no notion of longevity," the *Diamond Sutra* is actively building a world that is permanent, blissful, pure, and that has an independent self through the process of negation. Only when there is no self, no duality, no disputes, no suffering, and no barriers, can the permanent "true self" manifest.

⟨ 3 ⟩   "All great bodhisattvas should subdue their minds in the following manner: Of all sentient beings, be they born of eggs, wombs, moisture, or transformation, or whether they have form, or not form, or whether they are able to perceive, or do not perceive, or are neither able to perceive or not perceive, I cause them to enter *nirvana* without remainder, liberating them. Thus by liberating infinite, immeasurable, limitless sentient beings, in reality, no sentient beings are liberated."

"And why is this? Subhuti, if a bodhisattva has the notion of a self, the notion of others, the notion of sentient beings, or the notion of longevity, then he is not a bodhisattva."

When we give while attached to notions, we cannot gain great merit, just as when we attempt to liberate others while attached to the notion of self, we cannot develop compassion for those we liberate. Only when we develop great compassion that is unattached to the notion of self does it become possible to broadly liberate all living beings. There are many varieties of living beings, infinite varieties in fact. We should have no thought of discrimination when it comes to liberating living beings. We should generate an expansive aspiration to completely liberate all living beings.

> "Subhuti, suppose a bodhisattva gave a quantity of the seven treasures capable of filling as many worlds as there are grains of sand in the Ganges River; if a bodhisattva knows that all phenomena are without self and thereby attains patience the virtue he attains is superior. Subhuti, this is because all bodhisattvas do not receive this merit."
>
> Subhuti said to the Buddha, "World-honored One, why is it that bodhisattvas do not receive merit?"
>
> "Subhuti, the merit of a bodhisattva should not be attached to. That is why it is said that they do not receive merit."

In the sutras the Buddha sometimes refers to this world as the "Saha World," or *suopo* (娑婆) in Chinese, meaning "endurance." This world is called "endurance" because it is filled with affliction and suffering that we must endure in order to accomplish anything. In this instance, "endurance" also means patience: being patient with both the circumstances which support us and oppose us while remaining free from anger and abiding securely in the truth without being perturbed. Patience can be divided into three kinds: patience for life, patience for phenomena, and patience for the non-arising of phenomena. The phrase "attains patience" that appears in the above passage from the *Diamond Sutra* refers to patience for the non-arising of phenomena.

What is patience? Patience is recognition and acceptance. Patience is engaging in, dealing with, clearing up, and dissolving away. One example is when a father returns home and his son makes a fuss and says, "Dad, kneel down for me so I can play horsey!" and the father then really does kneel down to let his son ride on his back and play horsey. Not only is the father not offended, but he even laughs heartily because he loves his son; otherwise, he might have even given him a few slaps in the face.

Patience for life is recognizing the bitterness and sweetness of all life's experiences and the vagaries of interpersonal relationships, then taking responsibility for them and reconciling the affliction of past grievances. We must have patience for life if we hope to be able to sustain our lives and live freely. For example, if you have a job you may need to get up early in the morning to catch the bus, deal with the pain and exhaustion of sitting in traffic, put up with cold and hot weather, and endure lack of sleep. Once you get to work there may even be differences of opinion, favoritism, and grudges among your coworkers. Patience is the power of wisdom.

Patience for phenomena is coming to terms with the greed, hatred, delusion, and preconceptions in one's own mind by realizing that birth, old age, sickness, death, sorrow, pain, wealth and position, as well as transient human sentiment all arise and cease due to causes and conditions. The mind can find repose in this truth and no longer be affected by the arising and ceasing of those phenomena. Only by gaining insight into the inherent emptiness of dependent origination, is one able to gain the *prajna* wisdom that comprehends the principles behind phenomena and the nature of human emotion. For example, if someone curses me and calls me a bastard, I can laugh and think, "Ha ha, so I'm a bastard" or "Amitofo, thanks!" and not take offense. Then again, do I really become a bastard just because someone calls me that? Certainly not! This is transcending names and labels. By not stooping down to their level the person who utters the abuse becomes the bastard and not me. It is just as the *Sutra in Forty-two Sections* states:

> For the wicked to harm the virtuous would be like raising one's head and spitting at the sky; the spittle does not reach the sky, but falls back upon oneself. Or it is like throwing dust against the wind; the dust does not go someplace else, but collects upon oneself instead.

Patience for the non-arising of phenomena is the understanding that, fundamentally, nothing arises or ceases, for nothing inherently exists. Since all phenomena do not arise, in essence there is no need to be patient. This is the patience of non-patience. This is why bodhisattvas are not limited by the notion of merit, because bodhisattvas benefit living beings based on the aspiration for enlightenment rather than craving merit that may benefit themselves. Thus their generosity is free of attachment to notions. A noble bodhisattva who has attained patience and whose mind does not abide in phenomena will retain his virtue and it will not flow away, while a bodhisattva who is only concerned with giving treasures will have his merit flow away.

In the above passage the Buddha depicts several stages along the bodhisattva path. If a bodhisattva gives "a quantity of the seven treasures capable of filling as many worlds as there are grains of sand in the Ganges River," it is impossible to calculate the merit of such a gift. Bodhisattvas at this level know that external phenomena are not real, but they have yet to attain the patience of the non-arising of phenomena, because subtle traces of delusion still remain in their minds. Thus they give while attached to notions, and still lack the understanding of the doctrine of non-self.

However, a bodhisattva who understands that all phenomena lack an independent self, but instead are empty and arise out of causes and conditions, will be free from greed and have no need to acquire external things, nor will he be perturbed by the outside world. This is how the bodhisattva attains the patience of the non-arising of phenomena. By internally "abiding in the mind of non-abiding," the bodhisattva can then expand the Buddha's mission by liberating living beings with no notion of people, and attain Buddhahood with no notion of self.

After fully understanding "non-self" a bodhisattva no longer receives merit or yearns for *nirvana*, and is thus is said to be free from desire. When we say that they do not "receive merit" it does not mean that bodhisattvas reject the idea of cause and effect, but rather that they do not crave merit and are free from the type of delusion and discrimination which takes a calculating attitude towards accruing merit. A bodhisattva who has attained patience for the non-arising of phenomena means he is without a "self" and without notions. He is not attached to a sense of self, nor is he attached to the notion of giving or the notion of merit. This is what it really means to understand "all phenomena are without self."

One day a devotee came to see Chan Master Ikkyu and poured out his troubles:

"Master, I can't go on living," he said, "I'm going to kill myself!"

"Your life was going well, why would you want to commit suicide?"

"Oh master, ever since my business failed the debts have been piling up. My creditors are making it impossible for me to go on. Only death will put an end to it."

Chan Master Ikkyu replied, "Are you really telling me that there is no other way out except death?"

The devotee painfully said, "There isn't. I have nothing left except my young daughter. I have reached the end of my rope."

Chan Master Ikkyu had a sudden inspiration.

"Ah, I have an idea: you can marry your daughter to someone. Find a handsome, well-off son-in-law and he can help pay off your debts."

The devotee shook his head and said, "But master, my daughter is only eight years old. How can she marry anyone?"

"Then let me marry your daughter! I'll be your son-in-law and help you pay off your debts."

The devotee was shocked, "You...you simply must be joking! I revere you as my teacher, how can you become my son-in-law?"

But Chan Master Ikkyu had a plan. He waved the devotee off and said, "It will be alright. Nothing more needs be said: go home right now and announce the marriage. When the time comes to receive the bride, I will come to your house and become your son-in-law. Now hurry along."

This businessman-cum-disciple had confidence in the Chan master's wisdom, so he returned home and made the announcement at once: on such and such a date, Chan Master Ikkyu would be coming to his home to marry his daughter. As the news spread, it became a sensation throughout the city.

Finally the day to receive the bride came, and the area surrounding the home was packed so tightly with curious on-lookers that they could hardly move. Upon arriving at the scene, Chan Master Ikkyu gave the order that a table be placed in front of the gate with a writing brush, paper, an ink stick, and an ink stone. With a crowd in front of him, the Chan master wielded the writing brush, and as everyone marveled at how wonderful the master's calligraphy was, they jostled with one another to get a better view and buy his works. The crowd seemingly forgot all about why they had come in the first place. The upshot of all of this was that the money from people buying the calligraphy filled several baskets.

The Chan master turned and asked his devotee, "Is this enough money to pay off your debts?"

The devotee was so happy that he knelt down and bowed his head to the ground again and again, "Master, you are truly a miracle worker to have made so much money appear all of a sudden!"

Chan Master Ikkyu gave a sweep of his long, billowy sleeves and said, "Problem solved. I won't be your son-in-law after all, so I better remain your teacher. Goodbye."

Chan Master Ikkyu did not cling to the appearance of his own self-image, and for that reason alone he was able to liberate the devotee without attachment to the notion of self by applying skillful wisdom.

A Single Compassionate Thought

Once upon a time there was a man named Kandatta. He was a villainous person who was capable of all manner of terrible things. One day Kandatta was walking somewhere when he saw something black under his foot. He was just about to put his foot down, and crush what turned out to be a spider, but instead he experienced a moment of compassion.

"Why bother crushing it to death?" Kandatta thought. So he lifted his foot and stepped over it, saving the spider's life.

Kandatta was a remorseless criminal who did anything wicked, so upon his death he was condemned to Avici hell to experience unmitigated torment. But amidst his suffering a shiny, silver thread of spider's silk, as thin as steel wire, came floating down from the sky. Kandatta was like a man drowning in the ocean who had caught sight of a lifeboat, so he quickly grabbed hold of the spider thread and began to climb with all his might, wishing to be free from the uninterrupted pain of hell.

But once he looked down, he saw that the many other denizens of hell were climbing up behind him. Kandatta thought to himself: "How can such a thin spider's thread bear the weight of so many people? If the spider's thread were to break, then I will be trapped here for thousands of *kalpas* without any hope of being released."

So he thrust out his leg and started kicking those climbing up from behind off the thread one by one. Just then, the spider's thread snapped somewhere up above, and Kandatta along with the other denizens of hell all fell back into the bottomless blackness of hell to suffer its endless knife cuts and burning flames. With their physical eyes and desiring minds, living beings only see their own suffering and only think about their own liberation.

The story of the spider's thread is a very skillful teaching on the power of a single compassionate thought. Kandatta had a single thought of compassion towards a spider; however, while he was trying to save himself from Avici hell a single thought of selfishness doomed him to fall back into its hell's maw. A single dark thought is Avici hell, while a single compassionate thought to benefit oneself and others brings great good fortune. We exist in a relationship of oneness and coexistence, for all the world is one, and all things are interconnected through causes and conditions.

There Are None Who Cannot Be Liberated

I often like to say that any place can be a temple of enlightenment, and there is no one who cannot be liberated.

During the 1950s when I was teaching at Leiyin Temple in Ilan, Taiwan, there were always groups of people outside the hall laughing, talking loudly, and in many ways disturbing the people inside. One time I turned off all the lights, leaving only the glow of the burning incense in front of the Buddha statue. The noisy crowd outside was startled by the sudden and unexpected darkness and instantly fell silent.

Humanistic Buddhism is truly based upon liberating living beings without attachment to the notion of self. When teaching the Dharma, one cannot become attached to oneself or what is traditional. Once someone becomes attached to the Dharma, that person becomes rigid, formalistic, and cannot judge how the Dharma should be adapted to suit people's needs.

Once the Buddha gave the metaphor of practice being like tuning a musical instrument to one of his disciples who was formerly a musician, stating that he should not "tune" his mind too tightly or too loosely. The Buddha gave the metaphor of tending cows as similar to taming this restless body and mind to a devotee who was a cowherd. As a teacher, what the Buddha excelled at most was adapting his message to his students without clinging to notions, thus ensuring through skillful means that the wondrous Dharma connects with the minds of his listeners.

I have also tried to emulate the practice of adapting the Dharma to the needs of the people. For example, early on in Ilan I established the "Amitabha Buddha Recitation Society" to give illiterate people the chance to pick up the Buddhist sutras and recite for themselves, word by word, sentence by sentence. Next, in Ilan, I established Taiwan's first Buddhist choir. I wrote the lyrics to the songs, and I asked Yang Yungpo, a teacher at Ilan High School, to write the music. I then established a Chinese composition class for correcting students' compositions. At that same time I instituted after-school study sessions for underprivileged children and asked my followers who were teachers to volunteer their time as tutors in subjects like English, mathematics, physics, and chemistry.

In 1954 I stepped outside the temple by organizing a group to tour the island to publicize the recent printing of the Buddhist Tripitaka, the collection of canonical Buddhist texts, in Taiwan. I led my followers on a forty-four-day campaign all around Taiwan that taught the importance of the Buddhist Tripitaka. The campaign even reached as far as the distant island of Jibei in the Penghu Archipelago.

While giving lectures on the *Platform Sutra* in 1995, I invited the Taipei Chinese Classical Orchestra to perform in conjunction with my presentation. The orchestra played more than twenty pieces of music, including the "Buddhist Great Compassion Repentance Chant," the "Amitabha Buddha Recitation Suite," and "Buddhist Hymn with Bells," to lead the audience in singing verses from the *Platform Sutra*. In this way I was able to make the profound meaning of this sutra more accessible to modern people.

In 2002, I presided over a lecture series on Buddhist hymnal music at the National Dr. Sun Yat-sen Memorial Hall in Taipei.

These lectures combined narratives from Dunhuang literature,[1] Buddhist music, and liturgical chanting to meld literature and music. During the lecture series literature and art came together to act as an instrument for the Dharma to liberate living beings. We cannot allow the Dharma to become fixed, nor should we rigidly adhere to our own set ways of teaching. For as the *Lotus Sutra* says:

> Sentient beings have their various capacities:
> keen or dull, diligent or indolent;
> And [the Tathagata] teaches the Dharma to them
> According to their abilities.

The *Lotus Sutra* also mentions in its famous Universal Gate chapter:

> ...If there are living beings in this land who should be liberated by someone in the form of a Buddha, then Avalokitesvara Bodhisattva will manifest in the form of a Buddha and teach the Dharma to them.... For those who should be liberated by someone in the form of a lesser king, then he will manifest in the form of a lesser king and teach the Dharma to them.... For those who should be liberated by someone in the form of a young boy or young girl, then he will manifest in the form of

---

1. Dunhuang literature encompasses a corpus of ancient Chinese manuscripts discovered during the turn of the twentieth century in a series of underground caves in Dunhuang Province, China. The majority of the manuscripts are Buddhist texts, many of which were newly discovered, and are of intense interest to Buddhist scholars. *Ed.*

a young boy or young girl and teach the Dharma
to them.

In the same way, whenever artists come to Fo Guang Shan,
I talk with them about the cave murals at Dunhuang. When ath-
letes come, I talk about Shaolin gongfu. When farmers come, I talk
about how Buddhist monastics were the ones to first import certain fruits and vegetables from central Asia. When soldiers come,
I speak of how defending our country is like defending the mind.
When young students come, I talk about their future prospects.
When children come, I talk about what the sutras call the "four
small things not to be taken lightly": that a great fire can be caused
by a single spark, that the earth is nourished through single drops
of water, that little boys can grow up to be Dharma kings, and that
little girls can grow up to be Dharma queens. With members of the
National Science Committee, I can discuss the scientific qualities
of Buddhism. With members of the Ministry of Economics, I can
discuss the Buddhist view on wealth. With civil engineers, I can
discuss Buddhist architecture.

Since I am convinced that there is no one in the world who
cannot be liberated, I make a vow to do so, and then there is nothing that cannot be accomplished.

Generating an Aspiration

Liberating living beings without attachment to the notion of self
does not mean taking charge of another person's life or doing
everything for someone else. It means helping another person
to assume sole responsibility for his or her own life, career, and
spiritual practice, even in the process of liberating living beings.

To do this we must be able to supply for the various needs of living beings.

Having the aspiration to liberate living beings means more than giving them food when they are hungry and giving them clothing when they have nothing to wear. Such material exchanges and emotional interactions are bound to certain notions and are not long-lasting. To truly liberate living beings means to enable them all to enter *nirvana* without remainder, so that they can reach the state beyond birth and death. In order to liberate so many living beings and lead them to *nirvana* we must have an aspiration that is without duality. This is the only way to truly liberate living beings.

This skill is not one that can be mastered through learning, but can only be mastered through doing. Once we have generated the aspiration to liberate living beings we have limitless potential.

The *Encouragement for Generating the Aspiration for Enlightenment* by the Venerable Xing'an states:

> I once heard that generating aspiration heads the list of essential practices for entering the Buddhist path, while making a vow comes first among the urgent tasks for spiritual cultivation. When the aspiration is generated, then the Buddhist path can be accomplished; and when the vow is made, then living beings can be liberated.

The Dharma places value on what is practical. The secret to success is to have the will to get things done combined with responsibility and practicality. In order to have great aspirations we must have no notion of self. The less we involve our own "self," the greater the number of people we can contribute to, the less we feel our own attachments, and the more tolerant of others we become.

The early years at Fo Guang Shan were truly a difficult time, and manpower was in short supply. Even so, I had no qualms about my decision to send Tzu Hui, Tzu Jung, Tzu Chia, Tzu Yi, and Tzu Chuang to Japan to pursue advanced studies. Many people at the time would say to me, "If they go and make a life for themselves abroad and don't come back, you would be losing such talent, and would have wasted all your time and effort on them. But even if they do return, how could you lead such superior intellectuals?"

As it turned out, they did, indeed, return and helped Buddhism accomplish many things. There is an old saying in Buddhism, "Learning the Way can happen sooner or later, but each person has their special excellence." I have never felt that I was any smarter than my disciples. My hope has been that they will surpass me, just as the blue dye made from an indigo plant surpasses indigo in color.

In the *Diamond Sutra*, the Buddha reminds Subhuti not to be attached to the thought that "living beings can be liberated." This is because living beings are empty, and lack any real form. If we get caught up in thinking and assuming that living beings can be liberated, the we can become trapped by attachment to the notions of self, others, sentient beings, and longevity. This concept is explained in the following passage:

⟨ 25 ⟩ "Subhuti, what do you think? Do not say that the Tathagata has this thought: 'I should liberate sentient beings'. Subhuti, do not have this thought. And why is this? In reality, there are no sentient beings for the Tathagata to liberate. If there were sentient beings for the Tathagata to liberate, then the Tathagata would have a notion of self, others, sentient beings, and longevity."

"Subhuti, when the Tathagata speaks of a self, it is the same as no self, and yet all ordinary people take it as a self. Subhuti, the Tathagata says that ordinary people are not ordinary people, and that this is what is called ordinary people."

"No self" does not mean that we do not exist, but that we must not create a duality between ourselves and others. The *Flower Adornment Sutra* says that there is no difference between the mind, the Buddha, and living beings. There are three different ways of thinking about the self, which we will call the "soul," the "transient self," and the "true self." The "soul" is the misleading view of a permanent self put forth by many non-Buddhist teachings. The "transient self" is the false sense of self that ordinary beings cling to. The "true self" is the freedom of self realized by the Buddha.[2] The true self is the true nature of equality among all phenomena.

---

2. The "eightfold unimpeded self" consists of eight abilities possessed by the Buddha to expand the self beyond its normal bounds: (1) manifesting many bodies, (2) manifesting an infinitely small body that fills the universe, (3) manifesting a gigantic body that is so lightweight it can fly, (4) manifesting many forms in the same place, (5) using any sense organ as any other, (6) attaining all phenomena without the perception of having attained phenomena, (7) expounding the meaning of a single verse for countless kalpas, and (8) pervading all places like space itself. *Ed.*

The Buddha sees no distinction among the mind, the Buddha, and living beings, for all ordinary beings are endowed with the Buddha's wisdom. The designation "ordinary being" is but a temporary name, but what we call "ordinary beings" are just those who are attached to notions for a time and have not yet awakened. They have yet to gain realization into the cycle of birth and death. If, while liberating living beings, a Buddha were to generate the mental impurities of discrimination and partiality, then that Buddha would also become an ordinary person. When we are liberating living beings, we should do so without discrimination, and with a mind of equality, with no external perception that there are living beings to be liberated or any internal perception of a "self" that does that liberating.

It is ordinary beings with their sense of "self" that leads them to be attached to their own successes, and it is the fear that the successes of others will be higher than their own that creates discrimination and calculation. What such people do not realize is that a person's intelligence, abilities, wisdom, and accomplishments all come about through the combination of causes and conditions, and are actually the accumulated efforts of many people. Since our success comes about by the contribution of others, we also need not keep patting ourselves on the back when we help other people.

My disciples should not pursue advanced degrees for their own sakes, nor should they do so to make Fo Guang Shan a success. People should pursue education for the sake of the oneness, harmony, and coexistence of this world's living beings, and to be able to more effectively liberate sentient beings without attachment to the notion of self. This is why I let my disciples go abroad to pursue advanced degrees: so that they can broaden their minds, expand their vision, and give back to society what they have taken from it.

Now that I mention it, they are not even my disciples, nor are they the disciples of Fo Guang Shan. They are the disciples of Buddhism and of humanity. That is why, from the very founding of Fo Guang Shan, I established four "working principles" for our future endeavors. They are:

1. Give people confidence.
2. Give people joy.
3. Give people hope.
4. Render service to others.

Our hearts and minds are forever open to others and open to the world. By implementing these four working principles we can align ourselves with the *Diamond Sutra's* entreaty to liberate living beings without attachment to the notion of self and realize the *prajna* of true reality.

VI

Living

Without Abiding

 The mind of the past cannot be obtained,
The mind of the present cannot be obtained,
And the mind of the future cannot be obtained.

Where then does the mind reside?

Modern life is complex, and most people are switching the roles they play all the time. We've become attached to the six sense objects of sights, sounds, smells, tastes, touch, and dharmas, and worry each day about what we gain and what we lose. If we're not enjoying beautiful sights, then we're grasping at sounds and tastes. We mistake what is false to be true, what does not exist to exist, and what is defiled to be pure. We each find ourselves bewildered by our own delusional thoughts and the thoughts of others, and by the illusions of life and the world. We each have a heart and a brain, but as sentient beings, we are muddled in delusion, and our minds abide in the five desires and the six sense objects.

As long as the mind abides in something, it is not secure or stable. Sights, sounds, smells, tastes, touch, and dharmas will change. Once you make a sound, it no longer there; it is no longer yours. Yet if you do not abide in anything, do not engage in anything, and instead transcend all things, where will you abide? This is abiding in *prajna*, for it is something else entirely which transcends this world. However, even while abiding in the world of *prajna* one can freely interact with sights, sounds, smells, tastes, touch, and dharmas, for as human beings who live in the world we must have things like homes and families. It is possible to live like the great Buddhist layperson Vimalakirti, who is described in the *Vimalakirti Sutra* as "Though a layman, he is not attached to the three realms. Though married, he always cultivates purity."

When the Buddha became enlightened he didn't give up things like eating; he did not reject the world. He too lived in the world, and could become upset the same way we do, as well as scold others. But the Buddha's scolding is not the same as when an ordinary person scolds another. When the Buddha admonished his disciples, he would call them "ignorant of affliction," "deluded," or "inhumane." To me, this is scolding, but it is scolding done in a way that is artful rather than vindictive. When we get mad, our anger is followed by a surge of emotions, but when the Buddha was upset, he did not abide in his emotions. One such example is when the Buddha reprimanded his son, Rahula. It seemed that the Buddha was being very stern, but he was doing so to teach and reform his son. From here we can see that the Buddha was not fixed in his emotions, nor could he be manipulated by his emotions.

⟨ 18 ⟩   "Subhuti, what do you think, does the Tathagata have eyes of flesh or not?"

"Yes, World-honored One, the Tathagata has eyes of flesh."

"Subhuti, what do you think, does the Tathagata have heavenly eyes or not?"

"Yes, World-honored One, the Tathagata has heavenly eyes."

"Subhuti, what do you think, does the Tathagata have wisdom eyes or not?"

"Yes, World-honored One, the Tathagata has wisdom eyes."

"Subhuti, what do you think, does the Tathagata have Dharma eyes or not?"

"Yes, World-honored One, the Tathagata has Dharma eyes."

"Subhuti, what do you think, does the Tathagata have Buddha eyes or not?"

"Yes, World-honored One, the Tathagata has Buddha eyes."

"Subhuti, what do you think, has the Buddha said that the sand in the Ganges River is sand or not?"

"Yes, World-honored One, the Tathagata has said that it is sand."

"Subhuti, what do you think, if there were as many Ganges Rivers as there are grains of sand in the Ganges River, and if all of the sand in all of those rivers were added up, and if the number of Buddha worlds equaled the number of all of those grains of sand, would that be a lot?"

"It would be very much, World-honored One."

The Buddha said to Subhuti, "The Tathagata fully knows and fully sees the minds of the sentient beings in

> all of these worlds. And how can this be? The Tathagata
> has said that all minds are not minds and that thus they
> are called minds. And why is this so? Subhuti, the mind
> of the past cannot be obtained, the mind of the present
> cannot be obtained, and the mind of the future cannot
> be obtained."

In the above passage the Buddha uses the grains of sand in the
Ganges River as a metaphor for the great number of living beings
in existence, and yet the "Buddha eyes," which encompass all eyes,
are capable of knowing the mind of all living beings throughout
the various Buddha realms.

The *Treatise on the Awakening of Faith in Mahayana* contains
a highly influential passage that says "one mind opens two doors."
Living beings and the Buddha inherently have the same nature. It
is only because of delusion, the distinction between ignorance and
enlightenment, and the processes of arising, abiding, change, and
cessation that defilement and purity exist. "One mind opens two
doors" is a way of expressing this relationship: though the nature
of the mind does not change, the mind has both an aspect that
conforms to suchness and a delusional, conditional, and ignorant
aspect.

There is no inherent difference between living beings and the
Buddha, for the mind of a living being is the mind of the Buddha.
As living beings inherently possess Buddha nature there is fundamentally no distinction between them and the Buddha whatsoever. This is how the Tathagata is able to fully know and fully see
the nature of the minds of living beings.

Living beings have simply become muddled and deceived by
the six sense objects. They come up with all manner of deluded

thoughts and have forgotten the true mind, which is quiet and undisturbed. With such deluded thinking they cannot possibly gain insight into true reality.

The Buddha, however, is no longer affected by karma, and has become enlightened to the true mind. The Buddha knows that he is one with all living beings, and it is because of this oneness that the Buddha generated the compassion to liberate living beings by extinguishing their suffering with his compassion.

The "Buddha eye" mentioned in the above passage is said to encompass all kinds of vision, hence the expression "the same contemplation in oneness," which is "the myriad phenomena return to the one, for there is no other contemplation." In the same way as the one "Buddha eye" can encompass the five eyes, a single grain of sand encompasses all the sand of the Ganges River, one world encompasses many worlds, and one mind can encompass the minds of all living beings.

The five eyes mentioned in the above passage from the *Diamond Sutra* does not imply in any way that a person grow five pairs of eyes. The five eyes refers to five different states of vision that can be achieved with our eyes, through which we can see much more than our eyes normally can. The five eyes are:

1. Eyes of flesh: This refers to the type of vision that people in this world normally possess. This kind of vision can be halted by all manner of impediments.

2. Heavenly eyes: This type of vision is like that possessed by heavenly beings, though it can be obtained by ordinary people through meditation. Heavenly eyes allow one to see everything, whether indoors or outdoors,

day or night. This kind of vision is still hindered by misunderstanding of principles.

3. Wisdom eyes: This is the vision possessed by *sravakas* and *pratyekabuddhas*. It is vision imbued with wisdom, and is thus superior to the vision of heavenly eyes, but because of the obstruction of knowledge this vision lacks compassion. It is still inferior to the Dharma eyes, which provide vision with both wisdom and compassion.

4. Dharma eyes: This is the vision of bodhisattvas, and can adapt to any given circumstance to liberate sentient beings. With the vision of Dharma eyes, bodhisattvas perceive all worldly and transcendental phenomena in all their details, as well as the minds and karma of all living beings

5. Buddha eyes: The Buddha perceives the truth of all phenomena. Buddha eyes include the attributes of the four previous kinds of vision, but are far superior to them.

Again, there is no difference between the Buddha and ordinary people; the two are equal. Even though the Buddha possesses the "five eyes," he still possesses eyes of flesh like living beings. The five eyes can also be attained by ordinary people; ordinary people are only impeded by the assurance that their views are correct and their attachment to them. Because ordinary beings are still constrained by their biased views they cannot see all things thoroughly.

The *Flower Adornment Sutra* describes the mind of the Buddha in the following verse:

Pure in mind and free from all flattery and deceit;
Joyful by nature, delighting in compassion.

As long as we learn how to transform miserliness and greed into generosity, hatred into joy, and malevolence into kindness, then enmity and worry will be eliminated as a matter of course, and we will no longer find ourselves "licking honey off the razor's edge" in mad pursuit of the taste of the five desires.

Changing the external world is not as good as changing our own mental state. Consider how two people can feel differently about a pond full of fallen flowers: one person may feel pity that the fine flowers have lost their petals, while another may be happy that the fruit will soon be ripe.

There is a Buddhist verse by Fu Dashi that says:

Heavenly eyes are far-reaching and unimpeded;
Eyes of flesh are impeded and not far-reaching;
Dharma eyes only contemplate the worldly;
Wisdom eyes are directly aligned with emptiness;
Buddha eyes are like a thousand suns
Shining at different places with the same light;
Perfect illumination within the Dharma realm,
Where no place is left unrevealed.

The expression "dharma realm," *fajie* (法界) in Chinese, refers to the world of absolute reality that the Buddha has awakened to. The dharma realm is as vast as space, and within it there exists no mental distinctions; self and other are one and equal. All living beings can be seen as existing as living beings with the Buddha's own mind. When the mind is free from discrimination, it becomes like a flawless, bright mirror that can reflect anything that is but before it without obscuring it at all.

The discrimination created from illusory phenomena is abiding in notions. The *Diamond Sutra* says, "All forms are illusory," but if we can refrain from abiding in notions, then we will not be affected by these illusions. If we are not affected by illusions, then there is nothing that arises or ceases. In this way our pure intrinsic nature can manifest.

The mental state of "non-thought" is not obtaining the mind of the past, present, or future, and is also called the state of non-attachment. Only when we are free from attachment can our lives move forward rather than remaining in place like a spinning top. When we are free from attachment the mind does not abide in the six sense objects; it does not abide inwardly nor does it abide outwardly, but comes and goes freely. In pursuing the state of "non-thought" it can help to remember these three things:

1. Do Not Relive the Past

    As long as one's current life is better than the past there is no need to be attached to past glory. But so many people can be like old, white-haired ladies, reminiscing about bygone days. People get old and feel that they have lost their youth, that the years are adding up and that time is against them. This is when they sink into remembering the past, for looking back at bygone times can become a familiar habit. This is why one should not relive the past.

2. Do Not Desire the Present
   The many cravings and desires we encounter in this present life follow one after another. We should not get caught up in who is right and who is wrong, or worry about who wins and who loses. Once we begin to obsess about such things we start to discriminate and judge.

3. Do Not Fantasize about the Future
   The cycle of constant arising and ceasing is plagued by impermanence. The future has not yet arrived and already it is impossible to plan for the changes of impermanence. Since every moment is formed through a combination of causes and conditions it is impossible to guarantee what the future will bring.

This approach to the past, present, and future can be related to the Buddhist "threefold training" of morality, meditative concentration, and wisdom. In order to not relive the past, one can establish meditative concentration. To not desire the present, one should observe proper morality. To not fantasize about the future it is important to cultivate wisdom. The mental state of "non-thought" where the mind of the past, present, and future is not obtained is precisely the Buddhist threefold training.

The Mind of Pure Freedom

 10 The Buddha said to Subhuti, "What do you think? In the past, when the Tathagata was with Dipamkara Buddha, did he attain the Dharma?"

"No, World-honored One, when the Tathagata was with Dipamkara Buddha, he truly did not attain the Dharma."

"Subhuti, what do you say? Does a bodhisattva adorn the Buddha land?"

"No, World-honored One. And why is this? That which adorns the Buddha land is non-adornment, that is what is called adornment."

"For this reason, Subhuti, all great bodhisattvas should give rise to purity of mind in this way: they should not give rise to a mind that abides in form; they should not give rise to a mind that abides in sound, smell, taste, touch, or dharmas. They should give rise to a mind that does not abide in anything."

What is the largest thing in the world? In Buddhist cosmology there is a great mountain called Mount Sumeru that is said to be at the center of every world system, encompassing many realms. But Sumeru is not the largest thing. What is the fastest thing in the world? A lightning strike cuts across the sky in a fraction of a second, but lightning is not the fastest thing. A single thought can be much greater and much faster than either of these.

The distinction between something large enough that it can encompass the universe and something that is large enough to obscure a tiny speck of dust is merely a temporary label. In the above passage the Buddha attempts to remove for us various impediments like the notion that his enlightenment was predicted, the notion that he adorns the Buddha land, and even the notion that he attained enlightenment. To "not abide in anything" does not mean not accumulating merit and wisdom, nor does it mean having a nihilistic view that there is no such thing as predicting or attaining enlightenment. To "not abide in anything" means that we should affirm that the Buddha land does not need adorning, but is inherently and intrinsically complete, and that the Buddha's Dharmakaya is inherently dignified as well.

In the *Diamond Sutra* the Buddha says that there is no Dharma to teach, and no people who attain the Dharma, so that living beings can understand the empty nature of Buddhahood. Our minds, though they strive to attain, should not cling to any attainable phenomena. The mind that does not abide in anything is the mind of pure freedom.

During the late Tang dynasty there was a Chan master named Yunmen Wenyan who went to Zhejiang Province to seek instruction from Chan Master Daoming. As Yunmen entered the doorway of Daoming's hut, Daoming suddenly and forcefully slammed the door, pinning Yunmen's foot in the doorjamb.

Yunmen yelled, "Ahh! That really hurts!"

Daoming asked, "Who is it that is yelling in pain?"

"It's me, Yunmen!"

Daoming said, "And where do you feel pain?"

"It's my foot; you've got it pinned in the door."

Daoming asked again, "You say your foot is in the door, but where are you?"

"I'm outside."

Daoming continued, "If you are on the outside, how is it that your foot is on the inside?"

Yunmen then realized the profundity of what Chan Master Daoming was trying to express. There are no distinctions like "inside" or "outside" when it comes to the intrinsic nature of the Buddha or the inherent nature of *prajna*. Worldly opposites like inside and outside, you and me, good and bad, and even big and small are all fabrications. Sentient beings cling to labels and distinctions like "inside" and "outside" and get bound up in them, unable to transcend them.

When considering the inherent nature of the true mind, it can be said that negative karma is also empty by nature. When the delusional thoughts are extinguished, negative karma disappears as well. There is an old Buddhist saying that captures this sentiment: "Lay down the butcher's knife and become a Buddha here and now." Another Buddhist verse says:

> Wrongdoing is mind-made, originally empty;
> If the mind ceases, wrongdoing is extinguished.
> The mind, gone; wrongdoing, destroyed—both
>   are empty;
> This is called true repentance.

Every single thought contains within it all of the ten dharma realms. There is no telling how many times we traverse these ten realms in a single day. When we are compassionate and have the aspiration to attain enlightenment, isn't that the mind of the Buddha? When we give and serve others, isn't that the mind of a heavenly being? When we are greedy, hateful, or ignorant, and think about how we can get even with and harm, even kill, other people, is that not the mind of a hell-being, hungry ghost, or animal? Within the space of a single thought we can travel the entire universe. Without finding the true mind within this mess, we cannot possibly be free.

All sentient beings have their own attachments. For some it is fame, fortune, or positions of power. For others it may be beautiful clothing and romance. There are others who are attached to knowledge and opinion; such people may believe that science alone is rational and that Buddhism is superstition. However, when it comes to rational science, we can all agree that science, whether it be the laws of mathematics and physics or the experiments of chemistry and biology, must begin with a hypothesis. Surely these hypotheses from which all of our scientific understanding is derived are clear, understandable, and believable, right?

Sadly, this is not always true. Consider in plane geometry the hypothesis about whether or not two lines will converge when extended into infinity. It is impossible to prove such a hypothesis. How can anything be proven regarding infinity, let alone if two lines will intersect? But the proving of the hypothesis that two parallel lines do not intersect when extended infinitely is part of Euclidean geometry that so many have learned.

Another example is economics. Economic hypotheses are carried out under the assumption that all other factors will remain the same, but the conditions for this hypothesis will never exist in life. The only thing that is for certain is that everything is always changing! Isn't this the "impermanence" that we talk about in Buddhism?

If we consider where each theory begins, and think about all of the knowledge that permeates our everyday lives and social structures that we take for granted, can any of these theories stand up to examination?

Once Huineng was listening to Fifth Patriarch Hongren expound the meaning of the *Diamond Sutra*. When Hongren reached the passage "they should give rise to a mind that does not abide in anything," Huineng experienced a great awakening and realized that all phenomena are not separate from intrinsic nature. Huineng exclaimed excitedly:

"Who could have thought that intrinsic nature is inherently so pure and clear! Who could have thought that intrinsic nature is inherently neither created nor destroyed! Who could have thought that intrinsic nature is inherently complete! Who could have thought that intrinsic nature is inherently unmoving! Who could have thought that intrinsic nature can inherently manifest all phenomena!"

There are ten common epithets for the Buddha, one of the most common being *tathagata* in Sanskrit or *rulai* (如來) in Chinese. The meaning in both Sanskrit and Chinese is similar: *ru* means "thus" and *lai* means "come." This signifies that the Buddha cannot be said to have come from any concrete place, nor can he said to be going anywhere. Another way to analyze this name is that the first character, *ru*, represents what is called the Buddha's "Dharmakaya." That is the absolute aspect of the Buddha that pervades all of reality. The second character, *lai*, represents the Buddha's "Nirmanakaya." This is the aspect of the Buddha that manifests in various forms according to conditions to liberate living beings. By comparison, the Buddha's Nirmanakaya has hundreds of millions of different forms, while the Buddha's Dharmakaya is constant and unchanging. The combination of these two concepts into *rulai* creates a nondualistic relationship between what is in motion and what is still that is "thus as it is."

The intrinsic nature of living beings is inherently pure, and does not arise or cease. Human beings intrinsically neither come nor go, are not born, and do not die. Living beings are endowed with Buddha nature and need not seek anything outside themselves. Each person's intrinsic nature does not waver, and it is from this intrinsic nature that all phenomena arise.

Another way to explain the phrase "not abiding in anything" is to say "having no hypotheses." The Dharma tells us to have a mind that does not abide in anything, while science and the humanities ask that the mind abide in some particular thing. It is only because hypotheses abide in things that we can deduce the various theories and natural laws of science. The knowledge of science and the humanities could not possibly be established without such hypotheses. By not abiding in anything, the Dharma is able to undo the bonds that fetter our minds precisely because it need not rely on other causes or abide in hypotheses. This is the central meaning of the *Diamond Sutra*.

Prince Bhadrika was a cousin of the Buddha, who later joined the monastic order. On one occasion he was practicing in the forest with two other monastics, Aniruddha and Kimbila, when he began to shout, "Ah, such bliss; truly such great bliss!"

Aniruddha then asked him, "What are you shouting about? What has made you feel such bliss?"

Bhadrika replied, "Venerable Aniruddha, in the past when I was a prince, I lived in the royal palace with impregnable walls and battlements, and there were many attendants and warriors who stood guard over me with weapons in hand, yet I still was terrified of assassins plotting my murder. I ate the finest delicacies and dressed in silks and satins, living a life of extreme luxury, but during that time I never enjoyed the taste of my food, nor felt that my clothing was elegant enough. Now I have joined the monastic order. I have not a single bodyguard and am here mediating in the forest all by myself, but I do not fear that someone will come and kill me. My clothing and food are all quite simple, and yet my heart is full and content. I can now sit and sleep freely without the slightest feeling of unease. This is why I feel such bliss."

It is true that things like doting love, wealth, and positions of power may appear to bring happiness and comfort to life, but they can also be the burdens that shackle us.

When we give rise to a mind that does not abide in anything, this is our true Buddha nature. If we feel secure in our body and mind it becomes impossible for others to harm us with a look or try to entice us with some proposition. Neither poverty nor wealth, favor nor disfavor, honor nor disgrace can dissuade us from our original aspiration. If we want to find a place where we can settle down and be secure, we must be able to live without abiding.

A mind that no longer abides in anything takes a long time to cultivate. We must always remain vigilant and self-aware, and examine our aspirations to see if they are pure or impure, true or false. It is as the sutras say, "When your aspiration is true, the result will be perfect."

The mind is like empty space, and it should abide in nothing, just as the teachings indicate. There are a few phrases that I recommend people take to heart, that they may help us to learn to live securely with the mind as empty as space, so we can slowly learn to get along with this mind of ours. They are:

- The heat of summer and the chill of winter are both beautiful.
- North, south, east, and west are all fine.

- Whether high or low, up or down, both are wonderful.
- Nothing separates oneself and others.

Under Sentence of Death

The *Sutra on the Causes and Conditions of King Surupa* says:

> It is due to love that sorrow is produced;
> It is due to love that fear is produced;
> If there are those who are free of love,
> They will be without sorrow and without fear.

Confucius said, "When you love someone you want them to live, when you hate someone you want them to die." Love and hate are often entangled with one another. One day two people may love each other so much that they cannot bear to be apart, but the next day they might mix like fire and water. Now she hates him beyond all hatred, but she may still need his help in the future. When love and hate are present, the mind can never be free. Let me quote a poem by Su Manshu:

> This Chan mind has evoked jealousy
>   from the beauty;
> The Buddha said, in the end,
>   even our enemies are family.
> With bamboo hat and cape, I return,
> Without love or hate for anyone.

During the time of the Buddha, there was a young monastic who found it impossible to control his lustful thoughts towards the opposite sex, and this vexed him greatly. When he tried to meditate distracting thoughts would well up in his mind and he would no longer be able to concentrate on his practice.

One day this young monastic got to thinking, "If I cannot eliminate the affliction of such desires, these desires will destroy my morality. In order to preserve my pure morals and end suffering, I had better cut off my sexual organ. All at once I would feel peace and happiness, and be free from worry."

Just as the young monastic had found a knife and was about to do the deed, the Buddha walked in.

"Don't do such a foolish thing," the Buddha said. "The source of good and bad lies within the mind, not outside of it. You cannot eliminate the turmoil of your thoughts by seeking a solution outside the mind. You are not going to eliminate your afflictions that way."

In our lives we should simplify our desires, but the feeling of love is very strong. Human beings need love; love is after all the source of life. Without the love between our parents, how could we be born? Buddhists sometimes speak of a certain spiritual resonance, an emotional connection that is similar to how people say they "click" with one another. This too is a kind of love. If we did not have a certain love for the Buddha, how could we venerate him? If we had no love for our spiritual teachers, how could we treat them with respect? If we had no love for the temple, how could we be willing to work hard and make sacrifices for it?

This kind of love is a greater love than the love that comes from desire. This love is like the love we have for nature: we love the mountains, oceans, trees, and flowers; we enjoy being close to them but we do not need to possess them. On the other hand, desire is selfish and is derived from craving. It is always tangled with happiness and frustration. Pure love untainted by desire is very precious, for it can nourish and strengthen people without any selfish motivation or confusion. Love that seeks nothing and is always refined is compassion.

When the mind is tainted by and bound up with desire we experience sadness and fear, and we wander forsaken and alone amid the turmoil of the three realms. The *Diamond Sutra* instructs us to not let the mind abide in anything so that we do not develop desirous love, but instead can refine our love into the great compassion of giving.

Once there was a king whose beloved queen had fallen ill and died. The king was stricken with grief beyond all measure, such that he no longer ate or drank. Every day he would cry beside the remains of the queen, and though his many ministers would try to persuade the king to temper his grief and accept the queen's death, their words did not have the slightest effect.

Some time passed, until one day a sage visited the court. The king's ministers informed him of the situation, and the sage said to the king, "Your majesty, not only can I tell you in what realm your queen has been reborn, but I can make it so you can speak with her directly."

The king was overjoyed, and asked that he be brought to speak with his queen immediately. The sage then led the king out of the palace and pointed to the ground where two beetles were busy moving a piece of cow-dung.

"Your majesty," the sage began, "This is your queen who died not long ago. She has already been reborn as the wife of a dung beetle."

The king was stunned, "How dare you malign my queen?"

The sage responded, "Your majesty, you must believe me. Listen carefully."

The sage then called out to the beetle, and the king could hear the voice of his queen answer back. The king then asked the beetle, "Whom do you prefer? I, from your previous life, or your current husband, the dung beetle?"

The queen answered, "In my previous life I received your majesty's royal kindness and lived a happy life. But the past has faded like mist. Of course I now prefer my dung beetle husband."

Hearing those words, the king awoke as if from a dream. He then returned to his palace and ordered his ministers to bury the queen's remains.

There is an old Chinese saying that goes, "A speck of iron can obscure one's vision, but so can a speck of gold. Dark clouds may obscure the sun, but white clouds can also." Whether clouds are dark or bright they can still conceal the sun, and all chains can shackle us whether they are made of iron or gold. Both favorable and adverse circumstances are part of the Buddhist path. If good or bad situations are employed in the right way they can become skillful means to teach living beings. When we look upon the world we should do so in a way where we can look beyond the world, for only then can we be free from abiding.

Each day our lives fall more and more into a routine. So when the express train stops or volcanic ash disrupts air travel, we feel like the world has shattered and fallen into chaos. We become fixed in our habits and dependent on them, and this brings frustration and worry to our lives. For example, when we become accustomed to being loved by a certain someone, when that care and love are gone, we can become completely grief-stricken over the loss.

In ancient India there once lived a king who wanted to test just how strong the mind could be. One day he sent one of his ministers to the prison and told the minister to bring him one of the prisoners facing execution.

The king said to the prisoner, "You have been sentenced to death, but I will give you one chance to save yourself: I shall have placed upon your head a bowl filled with oil, which you may support with your two hands. If you walk down every avenue and street of this city without spilling a single drop of oil, I will pardon your crime."

The prisoner had been hopelessly awaiting his execution, and was overjoyed to be given this chance. He started to balance the bowl of oil on his head with great care and began walking the streets. The king attempted to distract the prisoner, and sent people to line the streets to showcase all manner of games and spectacles to the prisoner. He also chose the most beautiful women in the country to dance alongside the streets to melodious music right next to where the prisoner would pass.

The prisoner wanted nothing more than to live, and his only fear was that some of the oil would splash from the bowl he was balancing on his head. As such, he concentrated on every single step as he moved forward. All the beautiful sights and sounds were like a fog to him. None of it held his interest in the slightest.

Finally, the prisoner completed his circuit around the city and returned to the palace without spilling a single drop. The king asked, "When you were walking around the streets, did you not hear anything or see anything?"

"Not at all."

"Don't tell me you couldn't hear the pleasant music or see the appealing beauties?"

"Your majesty, I heard and saw nothing."

To have single-minded focus is to be like the prisoner balancing the bowl of oil on his head. It is complete and total concentration.

If we wish to live a life without abiding and be able to receive the unsurpassed Dharma of *prajna* we must be able to learn from the prisoner in this story: while trying to balance the bowl of oil in the mind we face the temptations of the five desires and must remain unmoved—looking but not seeing, listening but not hearing. We must protect the purity of the mind the same way the prisoner single-mindedly protected the bowl of oil balanced on his head. Then we will be able to go beyond life and death.

Where is the Mind?

Modern people are always multitasking: focusing their minds on many activities, believing that they can get more things done in the same amount of time. Some examples include using the computer while talking on a cell phone, or listening to music while eating a snack. With the mind dispersed between various activities in this way, we end up feeling very busy, and rather lost.

When we compiled all our forms of media including radio, television, newspapers, magazines, and now the internet, it seems like everyone is portraying themselves as some kind of expert. Everyone has advice on how to make more money than others, how to become successful before you turn thirty, how to keep up with the popular trends, or how to keep your finger on the pulse of the times and be on the leading edge. It seems like our mouths never stop, even for a moment, and just keep pouring out predictions, news of reconciliation and falling out, hearsay, and other rumors. There really is no need for each of us to add our own two cents, nor should we let such unexamined reports provoke quarrels and debate because off their wrongheaded ideas, words, and judgments.

There are many people who bury themselves in their work every day, and pressure others every second. They may pressure themselves, or let other people put pressure on them. People only turn to religion when they face disappointment and failure. This is treating religion like a cold remedy: once the cold is better, people go right back to their old ways and attitudes. Once again they become the same old person with all their bad habits. People can waste much of their lives repeating this cycle.

Once there was a man named Mr. Yin who devoted all his attention to becoming rich. Every day he would send his servants out on errands from morning until night and would never give them a moment's rest. One of his servants was an old man who was so tired from his labors that he would groan in pain. By evening he was drooping with exhaustion and each night he would sleep like a log.

In his sleep he would dream of being a king who enjoyed banquets and other amusements at the royal palace. In his dreams he could do as he pleased, for no one dared disobey him. But when he awoke the next morning he would be ordered about by the rich man as always.

Sometimes people would see the old servant work so hard and try to comfort him. The old servant would tell them, "A human life is no more than a hundred years; half of that is the day, and half of that is the night. During the day I am a servant and my work gives me a lot of hardship. But during the night I become a king and enjoy unequalled happiness. So why should I be concerned?"

Mr. Yin, the old servant's master, spent all his time thinking and scheming how to manage his family estate. All this effort left his body and mind completely exhausted, and he would collapse into bed each night dazed and weary. And as he slept he would dream that he was someone else's servant. He would run about here and there, carrying out endless labors. His master would scold, revile, beat, and humiliate him. Every night Mr. Yin would moan and groan in his sleep until morning.

The rich Mr. Yin was quite upset about this, so he asked a friend of his if there was anything he could do about it. His friend told him, "Your position ensures that you are honored by others. You are so wealthy that you could never spend all of your money, even given several lifetimes. During the day you're the boss, but at night you dream of being a servant. That sounds fair to me."

The world has always been a mixture of different parts. The *Treatise on Awakening of Faith in Mahayana* divides the mind into two aspects: the deluded mind that arises and ceases from moment to moment, and the true mind of emptiness, tranquility, and spiritual brightness that the deluded mind can gradually become. Vimalakirti, the great Buddhist layperson mentioned in the eponymous sutra, was said to frequent wine shops and gambling houses, though he would spend his time there employing skillful means to guide living beings. During the course of his many lifetimes of practice, the Buddha once saved the lives of five hundred merchants from the perils of piracy by not hesitating to break the precept against killing.

I sometimes call this world a "half and half world," because it is always part this and part that. Part of this world is the Buddha's world, and part of this world is Mara's world. Some teachings are right teachings, and some teachings are wrong teachings. That being said, there is an old saying in Buddhism that, "When the right person practices the wrong teachings, they become right teachings, and when the wrong person practices the right teachings, they become wrong teachings." We must choose what is wholesome and hold fast to it, planting ourselves firmly in the Buddha's world, and in the right teachings. We should not become bewildered and lead astray by Mara's part of the world, or by wrong teachings.

Even Buddhism is made up of different parts. Part of Buddhism is the "southern transmission," which is made up of countries of the Theravada tradition, while the other part is the "northern transmisson" which includes countries that practice Mahayana Buddhism. Buddhism is also made up of part "exoteric Buddhism" and part "esoteric Buddhism." One part of Buddhist practitioners are monastics, and another part are laypeople. I personally advocate drawing from both the northern and southern traditions, and fusing exoteric Buddhism with esoteric Buddhism. With the Fo Guang Shan Buddhist Order I have created a monastic order with a mature system, and with the Buddha's Light International Association I have organized a sound religious order for the laity.

Over the course of my life I have faced death many times. I have once had a medical operation where I experienced deep insight into the pain of illness at the point of life and death. Some people, even if their bodies are strong, may not recover when they fall ill. Other people may be in poor health and can suffer from many illnesses, but though their lives hang by a thread, they can live long, fruitful lives. There are some people who may have physical disabilities in one area, but function above average in another. Then again there are some people who may have a fair appearance and well-formed bodies, yet they look but cannot see, and listen but cannot hear; they are immoderate in their motions and askew in their demeanor. The world is always like this: nothing is ever entirely good or beautiful. Because of this we should not seek perfection, but instead see past such things and let them go. Then we can be free and joyous in any situation.

Every now and again I hear someone criticize Buddhism and say, "You Buddhists don't care about fine clothes and good food; you don't understand how to enjoy things and have fun. Isn't your life pessimistic and dull?"

But if that kind of happiness were real, why do so many people who live to enjoy such things feel that life is empty, and are left not knowing what to do? Why are there so many people who do not understand the meaning of this life?

In Buddhist writing we often use the expression, "I have Dharma joy and take no joy in worldly pleasures." Joy in the Dharma is the kind of joy that brings peace of mind and freedom, and harmony and serenity to our relationships. Look at all the people in society who only focus on obtaining fame and fortune. The only thing they know is the mad dash to be number one. They anxiously try and secure some personal gain from the material side of the world, while ignoring the spiritual side of the world. The more people jostle and try to squeeze through this one path, the narrower that path becomes; they end up getting battered and trampled into pulp. Life does not demand perfection. In everything, just do what you can do and you will not feel regret, wherever you may be.

Li Mi'an during the Qing dynasty wrote the poem "Half-Half Song" which best illustrates the sublime "half and half" state:

> Having seen through half of this transient life,
> Half of life is limitless enjoyment.
> The months and years with this half
>   have been completely carefree,
> Within this half, heaven and earth
>   are spread wide and clear.

A cottage in half town and
    half countryside,
A field that is halfway between hills and streams;
Half farming, half study, and half at home;
Relations that are half gentry and half common.
Utensils that are half refined and half coarse;
Rooms and courtyards being half elegant and
    half plain.
Clothing that is half plain and half novel;
Meal courses that are half sumptuous and
    half austere.
Servants that are half able and half clumsy;
A wife that is half simple and half talented.
Feeling half as a Buddha, and half as a deity;
My name is half hidden and half revealed.
I return half to heaven and earth;
And half I leave to the human world.
Half a consideration for posterity and
    future times;
Half a thought for how I will meet Yama,
    the lord of death.
Half tipsy with wine is just right;
Flowers when half open are quite the sight.
Boats with half sail the smoothest;
Horses with reins half-slacked ride the steadiest.
Half too little gives that extra taste;
While half too much is a wearisome burden.
Pleasure and pain have always been mixed
    half and half,
And those who gain the advantage are only half.

Chan Master Yaoshan once pointed to a pair of trees in the courtyard and asked his disciples, "Would it be better if these trees thrived or withered?"

His disciple Daowu said, "If they were to thrive it would be better."

His disciple Yunyan said, "If they were to wither it would be better."

The novice monk Gao said, "Let those that thrive thrive, and let those that wither wither."

What a good point: "Let those that thrive thrive, and let those that wither wither." In spring the red flowers and green leaves appear more striking because they are together, while at night the moon and stars both share their radiance. Such natural beauty gives us a powerful sense of the greatness of the universe. As long as we treat each other with respect and acceptance, maintaining a mutual harmony and balance, we will find that this world of "half this" and "half that" is truly wonderful.

In the Chan School of Buddhism, if you ask an old Chan master how he practices, he is likely to say, "Eating and sleeping."

Now, you may think, "Don't we eat and sleep too? Are we also practicing well?" But that kind of eating and sleeping does not count. When an ordinary person eats, he picks the lean or chooses the fat, and when an ordinary person sleeps he tosses and turns without sleeping peacefully. When an old Chan master eats, even the vegetable stalks are tasty, and when he sleeps he is comfortable and peaceful. It is not the same.

What is spiritual practice, really? If we take eating as an example, if you can find every meal delicious and tasty, then this is meditative bliss and Dharma joy. If you can sleep comfortably and at ease, that is liberation. Feeling peace in your heart is spiritual practice.

Chan Master Dazhu Huihai once said, "Eat when hungry and sleep when tired." Being able to sleep soundly without abiding in thought requires that we cultivate good karma. Let us take insight from this laudatory verse in the nineteenth chapter of the *Mahaparinirvana Sutra*, the "Chapter on Pure Practice:"

> If one's body is free of all negative karma,
> And in speech one turns away from the four wrongs,[1]
> Then the mind will not be entangled in doubts,
> And one will be able to sleep peacefully.

> If the mind and body can be unperturbed,
> Abiding securely in a place of tranquility,
> Then one obtains unsurpassed bliss,
> And one will be able to sleep peacefully.

> If the mind has no clinging attachments,
> Keeping far removed for all enmity,
> Then be always harmonious and free of struggles
> And one will be able to sleep peacefully.

> If one does not create negative karma,
> The mind always keeping a penitent attitude,
> Then trust that wrong will meet its due,
> And one will be able to sleep peacefully.

> Respectfully care for one's parents,
> Do not harm a single life,

---

1. The four kinds of wrong speech: lying, duplicitous speech, harsh speech, and flattery. *Ed.*

Nor steal the property of others,
Then one will be able to sleep peacefully.

Subdue all the organs of sensation,
Draw near good spiritual friends,
And destroy the hosts of the four Maras,[2]
Then one will be able to sleep peacefully.

Therefore, we should not bring our frustrations to bed. Any unhappiness that happened today, we should let go of. Do not take them with you when you sleep, and do not carry your anger and resentment into tomorrow. If you want to live a life in which you practice without abiding, then you must not keep your anger overnight.

Meditation means turning off the self that abides in things; it means breaking out of the daily routine of abiding. One no longer clings to delusional thoughts and biased attachments, but brings the mind back to the pure *bodhi* of the freedom of non-abiding.

There is a saying in the Chan tradition: "Without a meditation breakthrough, do not dwell in the mountains." We can see that the bodhisattva's practice depends upon the cultivation of both merit and wisdom. We can only speak of dwelling in a mountain retreat after our minds have had some kind of achievement. But meditative attainment should not lead to arrogance or be used to mislead others and deceive ourselves. Meditation retreats are not an escape from life, nor should they degenerate into a stepping stone for advancement and notoriety. True sitting meditation during retreat must achieve the following:

---

2. These include Mara as the deity who is an adversary of the Buddha, but also encompasses our afflictions, the five aggregates,and the cycle of birth and death. *Ed.*

- It should shut out the thieves of the six sense organs.
- It should forbid the mind from straying to delusional thinking.
- It should correctly contemplate the armies of the three poisons.
- It should purify the karma of body, speech, and mind.

"Sitting meditation" does not just mean superficially sitting quietly on a meditation mat. Sitting meditation is where we can transcend all things, such that the mind is no longer disturbed. Through sitting meditation one can fully understand the mind and see intrinsic nature. By seeing intrinsic nature, one attains emptiness, and emptiness is itself *prajna*.

Time Management

Those who have read up to this point may get the feeling that the freedom and independence that comes from having a "mind that does not abide in anything" means just living a free and easy life; that we can do whatever we feel like doing while being relaxed and carefree, without any need to manage our time.

But that is not the case. For myself, whenever I do something, I do pre-event planning and use my spare time in a suitable manner. When I have appointments with other people, I make sure to account for any errors in timing into the trip. Why? Because keeping my word is more precious than time. Excuses such as being busy or not having enough time should not be used to leave others waiting too long. It often happens that I am already sitting patiently in the car while my disciples who are accompanying me are scattered about, delaying the trip. I've said to them many times, half as a reprimand and half in jest, "I'm spending my whole life waiting like this!"

When I need to tape something for a television broadcast, I am always well prepared beforehand, regardless of whether the episode is five minutes or eight minutes long. I work out the opening, expansion, development, and conclusion for each topic, and when I finish speaking my timing is never off by more than fifteen seconds. I have never flubbed a scene. The tape can always be broadcast as is without any editing.

Time management is how we cherish our own life. For people who manage their time and use it well, their time is spiritual time. When people do not manage their time well, their time ends up merely being the time as marked by clocks and watches.

Not Abiding in Positions of Power

Early on after Fo Guang Shan was founded, we drafted a series of bylaws. Article 4, Item 22 reads as follows:

> The abbot of this temple is the head of the religious order and serves for a term of six years. If reelected, the abbot is allowed to serve one consecutive term. Under special circumstances, and with two-thirds or more in agreement, the abbot is allowed to serve a second consecutive term.

As my second term as abbot was about to expire, I had already begun deliberations on a successor, and when my third term expired, I announced I was stepping down as abbot in accordance with the bylaws. Many devotees came and pleaded with me, asking me to stay, but my mind was already made up. In 1985 I turned the position of abbot over to the Venerable Hsin Ping.

I began serving as abbot of Fo Guang Shan at the age of forty, and those that followed, the venerables Hsin Ping, Hsin Ting, and Hsin Pei, all took up the position around the age of forty, while the new group of Religious Affairs Committee members were all from the "younger generation."

The transition of leadership for any nation, enterprise, or organization is the real linchpin for sustained management. As long as human beings are involved, we cannot avoid the "win or lose" mentality. The more we get caught up in it, the heavier burden we bear. We should all look upon stepping in or out of office with indifference, because unless we are able to let it go, we cannot live a transcendent and carefree existence.

Do not stay too long in positions of power; give the young people a chance and let them do the job. If they cannot do it well, we, the somewhat more experienced and qualified, will still be around to call for correction and pass on our experience.

Freedom from Life and Death

The Chan Master Damei Fachang knew that he would soon pass away, so one day he said to his disciples: "As for what is about to come, we cannot possibly resist it, nor can we possibly detain what has just passed even for a moment!"

Chan Master Damei Fachang was composed and fearless. Just as he was about to close his eyes and depart from this world, he heard the call of a squirrel outside the window.

The Chan master smiled and said, "What practitioners pursue all their lives is this present moment. Nothing else. You should all practice hard, for I will leave you now."

The moment before his *nirvana*, Chan Master Damei Fachang only heard the call of a squirrel—nothing else. Within that sound is contained all phenomena, and yet there is nothing within it. Not abiding in life and death is applying *prajna* to transcend life and death. Not abiding in *nirvana* is applying great compassion to serve humanity and liberate living beings.

The *Perfection of Great Wisdom Sutra* describes great bodhisattvas as being free from any attachment to *nirvana*, and thus being able to move from the shore of birth and death to the other shore of *nirvana*. If a great bodhisattva had even the slightest attachment, then he would be unable to go from this shore to the other shore.

The Japanese Chan Master Taigu Ryokan entered *nirvana* on January 6, 1831. Just before he passed away, he said that death was just like going to sleep, and that the most wonderful moment of all was when death came. He instructed us to not abide in the past, present, or future, and that only by enjoying death's tranquility with no-mind can we enter the Buddhist path. He left behind the following verse:

> Signs of spring are on the branch tips;
> The cuckoo calls deep in the mountains.
> Red leaves swirl away in the wind,
> Leaving nary a sign or trace.

Ordinary people often are afraid of the uncertain future, feel regretful about the past, and cannot be present in the now. We often have mixed and confused feelings about the present moment. We worry that the good times will not last, and blame ourselves for the past when we are feeling depressed. Sometimes people will go crazy and contemplate suicide, and other times wish that they could live forever. Sentient beings are always thinking this way and that, back and forth. Their minds are like wild horses that stir up clouds of dust wherever they go.

During the final years of the Tang dynasty the Daoist Lü Dongbin took the imperial examination on three occasions but failed each time. By chance he met the Daoist Zhong Liquan in a small wine shop, and Zhong Liquan passed on to him the magic art of prolonging life. From that point onwards, Lü Dongbin turned away from public life.

One day as Lü Dongbin was passing Mount Huanglong, he saw purple clouds billowing above the mountain, and he knew that some extraordinary individual must be there, so he went there to visit him. As Lü Dongbin entered the hall and joined the crowd, Chan Master Huanglong was beating a drum.

Chan Master Huanglong saw Lü Dongbin as he entered and later shouted, "There is a thief here stealing the Dharma!"

Lü Dongbin stepped out of the crowd, faced the Chan master, and recited a couplet:

"'A grain of rice contains the world; a small pot can cook the earth.' Can you tell me what it means?"

Huanglong said, "You are nothing more than a ghost that will not leave its own dead body."

Lü Dongbin said, "You have nothing that can compare with my elixir of immortality."

Huanglong replied, "Even if you live for countless thousands of years, you will end up with nothing."

These words frightened Lü Dongbin, so he threw a sword directly at Huanglong, but the blade could not pierce his skin. Unable to harm Huanglong, Lü Dongbin knelt down and asked Huanglong to teach him.

Huanglong said, "I will not ask you about the pot that can cook the earth, but what is this grain of rice that can contain the world?"

Lü Dongbin was suddenly enlightened, and thereafter wrote the following verse:

> Casting away the gourd elixir bottle, smashing
>   the lute,
> I no longer yearn for the alchemy of metal in
>   water.
> As soon as I met with Huanglong and ever since,
> I began to realize how my previous efforts were
>   all wrong.

Lü Dongbin threw away his elixir of immortality, for he now realized that, for a long time, he had been clinging to his physical body and wasting his mental energy. Even if one's physical form can persist for over one hundred million *kalpas*, it will still degenerate in the end. This physical body is merely a combination of the causes and conditions of the four great elements. Why must we wrack out brains trying to sustain it?

Everything in the world arises and ceases through a process of formation, abiding, decay, and extinction. Death is not only something that happens to our bodies, but can also describe the arising and ceasing of each thought. When fame and fortune die, when love dies, when our reputation dies, when our power and influence dies, or when any such thing comes to an end we are left feeling like we have nothing to rely on. We must develop a deep understanding of how causes and conditions work, for arising and ceasing do not inherently abide in anything, and only when we understand this can we remain carefree as conditions arise.

At the beginning of the chapter on Contemplating Causality in the *Treatise on the Middle Way* there is a poem called the "Hymn in Praise of the Eightfold Negation Causality," which can explain how the essence of the Dharmakaya lacks the delusional notions of arising, ceasing, eternity, nothingness, sameness, difference, coming, or going:

> Not arising and not ceasing;
> Neither eternalism nor nihilism;
> Not the same nor different;
> Not coming and not going;
> Is how causality can be described,
> Which excels at demolishing all sophistry.
> I bow in homage to the Buddha,
> For this is foremost among all his teachings.

Life is connected to death and death is connected to life, for what has life will die and after death there is life. Life and death have always been but temporary states of existence. What is the use in worrying about them? Why not be free?

To live without abiding means not letting external things determine our happiness, nor the self determine our sadness. It is to live by transcending external circumstances and not clinging to one's own mind. What the Buddha reveals in the *Diamond Sutra* is not a set of mysterious principles beyond this world, but rather how ordinary people can illuminate the intrinsic nature of *prajna* in their lives, and thus live a freer existence.

Life and death are both parts of this world. If we only see life, then we will be happy as a lark; but if we only see death, then we will be miserably sad. Whether we only focus on life or death, only seeing one part of the world makes us unable to appreciate that the cycle of life and death is like a flame being passed from candle to candle without pause. Indeed, life and death are not two separate things at all: Life is not truly life, and death is not truly death, for our lives are unborn and undying.

Buddhist practitioners are experts at understanding life and death. While it is said that the life between each breath cannot be known and that the present moment is impossible to control, we must master each and every thought and clearly understand the value of the spiritual world. This understanding can allow us to cherish the things and feelings of our world even more, and to develop determination to build a pure land of truth, goodness, and beauty.

VII

Cultivation

Without Attainment

<blockquote>
22

Subhuti said to the Buddha, "World-honored One, the Buddha attained *anuttara samyaksambodhi*, yet nothing was attained?"

"So it is, so it is, there is not even the slightest Dharma that can be attained in *anuttara samyaksambodhi*, and this is what is called *anuttara samyaksambodhi*."
</blockquote>

In the above passage Subhuti uses the phrase "nothing was attained" to say that the Dharma is not fixed, and in that sense cannot be attained. We all inherently possess the wondrous Dharma of *prajna*; it is not something that can be attained outside of the mind. We never lack it in the first place, so we cannot say that it is gained. One who believes that there is something to be attained still has attachments.

An ordinary person may believe that there is something to be gained or that the Dharma can be fully described in words, but each of these is a form of attachment and constitutes "abiding in something." Then there are others who believe that the Dharma cannot be described, nor is there anything to gain; however, they do think the mind can be obtained. Both of these views lead to clinging and attachment, causing one to face both phenomenal hindrances, and principle hindrances. "Phenomenal hindrances" are the phenomena which hinder ordinary beings, while "principle hindrances" are the errors in understanding that hinder bodhisattvas. The realization that "nothing is attained" breaks through phenomenal and principle hindrances, and the understanding that the Dharma cannot be fully explained in words breaks through the hindrance of language. In this way, "non-attainment" is the only true attainment, and is what allows us to return to our intrinsic nature, which is inherently pure.

In the *Diamond Sutra*, the Buddha says, "That which is called the Buddhadharma is not the Buddhadharma." In the *Diamond Sutra* the Buddha negates one teaching to establish another, and establishes one teaching to negate another. Whether he is constructing or negating, the Buddha does not want us to abide in any teaching, so that we can realize our intrinsic *prajna* nature.

One day, Chan Master Tianran suddenly told his disciples, "I miss the mountain forest. I wish to live there for my remaining years." The Chan master then put an end to his life of wandering and built a small hut on Mount Danxia in Nanyang County, China. Within three years, people began to come in droves to seek instruction from Chan Master Tianran, and his disciples grew to number three hundred. As a consequence, his simple hut expanded and became a temple complex.

Chan Master Tianran would often say to his disciples, "Safeguard well that thing of yours; for it cannot be spoken of. Can Chan really be explained? And how is this so-called Buddhahood to be realized? I have disliked hearing that word 'Buddha' my entire life. These days Buddhists scramble about and busy themselves with meditation and the search for enlightenment, yet they do not realize the treasure they possess. I can offer no path to cultivate here, nor Dharma to realize. Realize your mind, and there will be no worries or concerns. Fail to realize your mind and you will be deluded about your own intrinsic nature. Such is like the blind leading the blind, who altogether jump into a fiery pit."

Chan Master Tianran was attempting to eliminate ordinary beings' hindrance of believing that there is some correct realization that can be attained. He was also attempting to eliminate the principle hindrance of having fixed ideas and preconceived notions: when we think to ourselves that we understand enlightenment, or even that we have realized enlightenment, we can end up with very fixed ideas about everything. We may even start comparing our knowledge and practice with that of others, trying to see who comes out on top. This is when our practice can actually become an obstacle for us. That is why we should try to practice not to gain anything. However, *prajna* allows us to transcend the knowledge and wisdom that can act as obstructions. It is only by having a mind that does not abide in anything that all of wondrous existence is able to arise from emptiness.

When National Master Muso Soseki was a young man, he traveled a great distance to come to Kyoto to learn from Yishan, a Chinese Chan master who taught in Japan. One day, Muso went to see Yishan and formally asked for instruction in the Dharma by saying, "Your disciple is still unclear about the great matter.[1] Master, I beg you to teach me how to realize enlightenment."

Yishan replied, "In our tradition there is nothing to say, so how can a single word of instruction be given?"

---

1. A common Buddhist expression found in the *Lotus Sutra* to refer to the problem of life and death. *Ed.*

Muso pleaded again and again, "Master, please teach me with your skillful means of compassion."

Yishan answered in a much harsher tone, "I have no skillful means, and no compassion either!"

Having been rejected by Yishan so many times, Muso thought that he must not have a good karmic connection with Yishan. He resolved to leave Yishan's monastery and head to Manju Temple in Kamakura to request the teachings from Chan Master Koho Kennichi. Koho Kennichi would beat and shout at him mercilessly, causing even more pain to Muso who was so firmly committed to seeking enlightenment. Brokenhearted, Muso vowed to Koho Kennichi, "Until your disciple has extinguished all delusion, I will not return to see you."

Muso then went off by himself into the mountain forest where he practiced hard day and night, contemplating in quiet solitude.

One day Muso was sitting under a tree. A faint breeze was blowing softly and his mind was as still and quiet as a mirror. The day had drawn to midnight without him realizing it, and it was soon time for him to rest for the night. Just before he was about to go to bed, he reclined slightly to lean against a wall when, to his surprise, he fell over. It turned out there had never been a wall there against which he could lean, He had only thought there was. The moment he fell over, Muso unconsciously let out a laugh and suddenly attained enlightenment. He then spontaneously composed this verse:

> Many years digging in the ground looking for
> the blue sky;
> Adding layer upon layer of things obstructing
> my heart.

A common brick comes flying in the darkness
one night,
Casually breaking the bones of empty space.

There is no wall to lean on, even though some people may believe there to be. Some people are unwilling to cultivate their diamond-like mind, or see their intrinsic *prajna* nature. Some people believe that they can attain enlightenment and live a life of freedom by relying on others or following some sort of set formula. To believe this is blind faith, and to maintain it is superstition. National Master Muso Soseki attained enlightenment at the age of thirty-one, and the conditions that brought him to enlightenment stemmed from the kindness of the Chan masters who used their rough treatment of him as a skillful means. They did not want him to become attached to language nor to the notion of the Dharma, for the *prajna* mind lies directly within our own minds.

No Attainment, But Not Negating Attainment

One morning, the Buddha put on his robe, picked up his bowl, and went into the city of Sravasti to beg for food. Ananda accompanied him. That morning they saw an old couple, their backs stooped over, who were warming themselves over some burning garbage. They looked like a pair of old cranes missing all their feathers, and they displayed a greedy and miserable expression.

The Buddha told Ananda, "If this old couple had scrimped and saved in the past, they could have become wealthy elders of Sravasti. If they had cultivated the spiritual path with unrelenting zeal, then they could have become arhats, or non-returners, or once-returners, or stream-enterers,[2] thereby becoming noble ones and attaining the bliss of liberation. But when they were young, they were lax and extravagant. They did not put effort into attaining a comfortable living, they heard the Dharma but did not uphold and practice it, and they did not live in a pure and upright fashion. That is why, in their old age, they are like old cranes that have landed on the banks of a dried up pond. The only thing they can do is spend their remaining years of life in such misery."

While we say there is "nothing to attain," this does not negate the attainments of spiritual practice. The Buddha wants us to cultivate free of attachments, but that does not mean that we do not need to cultivate. There are some people who will chant the sutras, bow to the Buddha now and then, and perform various acts of giving, but when they meet with the slightest difficulties regarding their emotions, career, work, or health, they blame the Buddhas and bodhisattvas for not protecting them. The Dharma is not some business deal. As we interact with the Buddhas and bodhisattvas our faith should increase and become more pure. We should be able to feel connected to all the Buddhas, rather than always putting up roadblocks. If in our minds we are looking to get something, how can we be free?

Once there was a particularly zealous Buddhist practitioner who made his own Buddha statue. Every day he would carry the statue with him and devoutly make offerings to it. One day this practitioner went to a Buddhist temple to burn incense, but noticed that the incense he was burning wafted off to the other Buddha statutes. He thought to himself, "My Buddha statue cannot smell the incense I burn. I need to fix this."

---

2. These are four levels of great spiritual attainment, with the arhat being the highest. The non-returner, once-returner, and stream-enterer are each assured to become arhats in a varying number of future rebirths. *Ed.*

He soon came up with an idea: he would drill holes in the nostrils of his Buddha statue to which he could affix some incense, and that way only his Buddha statue would enjoy the incense he burned.

A few days later the practitioner's Buddha statue, originally immaculate and clean, now had its nose blackened by the smoke. Only then did the practitioner realize that his own delusion had ruined the majestic appearance of the Buddha statue.

Not Alarmed, Not Frightened, Not Scared

The mind that abides in no one thing is then able to abide as conditions arise and change, protecting us from the many snares of karma. When the mind abides in things, it cannot recognize wisdom, and its attachments make it impossible for us to get a clear handle on life's priorities. Only a mind that does not abide in anything is not alarmed, frightened, or scared, and is thus free from distortion and delusion. As long as the mind is seeking something, our faith, too, will become distorted.

 The Buddha said to Subhuti, "So it is, so it is. Moreover, if a person hears this sutra and does not become alarmed, or frightened, or scared, then this person is indeed a rare person."

What does the Buddha mean when he says "not become alarmed, or frightened, or scared"? The great master Sengzhao offered the following explanation:

Having attained the Mahayana wisdom through listening, one consistently listens to the teachings and one's body will show no sign of fear; so it is called being "not alarmed." Having attained the Mahayana wisdom through contemplation, one experiences a deep faith without any doubt; so it is called being "not frightened." Having attained the Mahayana wisdom through cultivation, one cultivates the practice according to the teachings, and one will never be maligned; so it is called being "not scared."

The Buddha says that, if upon hearing the *Diamond Sutra* people "believe it and [do] not turn their minds against it," their merit will exceed that from the giving of their lives countlessly over a period of countless eons. "Believing it and not turning the mind against it" means being able to receive and uphold the wisdom written in the *Diamond Sutra*. The mind not abiding in any single place will not produce calumny. By receiving, upholding, reading, and chanting the *Diamond Sutra*, one is able to benefit oneself, and by explaining it to people, one is able to benefit others. In his *Exegesis on the Diamond Sutra* the Sixth Patriarch Huineng states:

The faithful are obedient to principles, and so the text says "not turning against it." Practice and understanding in accord with one another is known as "receiving it"; determination and diligence are known as "upholding it"; the undistracted mind is known as "reading it"; and seeing nature and not turning against it is known as "chanting it."

The *Vastly Profound and Gloriously Pure Non-Retrogressing Dharma Wheel Sutra* states:

> Ananda, the faith of a great bodhisattva is pure, for there is no faintheartedness. They attain a pure mind with respect to the Buddha, Dharma, and Sangha. They watch over their six sense organs and want for nothing. They cause living beings with no faith in the Buddha, Dharma, and Sangha to generate the joy of faith. With the joy of faith generated, the mind will not be self-indulgent; and when generating the aspiration for enlightenment, one will not cling to mental notions. Faith brings the realization that the six great elements[3] are equal to the dharma realm.

Those who practice the bodhisattva path are able to maintain a faith that does not regress. They are naturally harmonious and meek. There is no faintheartedness for they are in want of nothing. They enter the ocean of the Triple Gem and receive the treasure of wisdom capable of fulfilling all their wishes.

The faith of ordinary people is fragile, and hearing examples of people with good intentions who are not rewarded may cause them to question the Dharma. Such people believe in the Dharma one day and then doubt it for three. This is not unlike a fisherman who fishes for three days and then dries his nets for five. Such people are ignorant and, even if they wish to be enlightened, will not become enlightened.

---

3. Earth, water, fire, wind, space, and consciousness. *Ed.*

Once there was an old monk who wished to raise funds to build a temple, so he would spend his days chanting sutras and reciting Amitabha Buddha's name at the town market, hoping for donations.

Three months went by and no one took any notice of him. Near the monk's spot in the town square there was a boy who sold wheat cakes who became quite incensed by what he saw. The boy thought to himself, "Gosh, that old monk is really having a rough time. I'll give him the money I get from selling these wheat cakes."

So the boy took the money obtained from selling wheat cakes that day and donated the entire sum to the old monk. When the people at the marketplace heard that the boy selling baked wheat cakes had made a donation, they felt ashamed. One merchant considered, "If a mere boy selling wheat cakes knows about cultivating merit, how can I not be as good as him?"

The news passed from one person to ten, then from ten to one hundred, and in short order the old monk secured all the funds needed for building the temple. The old monk was extremely grateful for what the boy had done, and he said to the boy, "Child, today you have shown such kindness and generated great merit. If you experience any sort of hardship in the future, remember to come to the temple to see me."

After heading back, the boy was fired by his boss because he could not turn over the money from selling wheat cakes. Unable to find another job, the boy wandered the streets and was eventually reduced to begging. He often went hungry, contracted scabies, and eventually went blind. One day, the boy remembered what the old monk had told him, and step by step he groped his way to the temple.

The old monk was a great cultivator, such that he had already developed heavenly eyes, and thus knew the boy's predicament and that he was coming to the temple seeking aid. So that night he gathered the monks together and explained, "Tomorrow our temple's great Dharma protector and benefactor will be coming. Everyone should gather at the temple gate to respectfully receive this guest. We must show him great hospitality."

The next day the entire temple staff had swept the place clean and was awaiting the benefactor's arrival. But the morning became late afternoon, and no such person had shown up. The old monk sent someone to inquire about the matter and the receptionist replied doubtfully, "No great Dharma protector and benefactor has made an appearance today."

The old monk made a further inquiry, "You mean to say that no one has been by today at all?"

The young monk then spoke haltingly, "No, there was no one. Well, there was only one little blind beggar, that is all. He wanted to come in, but I was afraid he would spoil the great welcoming ceremony you had planned, so I gave him a few pieces of bread and sent him on his way."

The old monk shouted, "That was our great protector and benefactor! Hurry and bring him back!"

Although some reluctance showed on the monk's faces, no one dared disobey, so all they could do was leave the temple and start searching. Fortunately the blind boy walked slowly, and so it was not long before they caught up with him. The young boy was welcomed back into the temple and given a room, where he was treated with the utmost respect and cared for in every possible way. But no one could have imagined that one night, as the boy went to the latrine, he accidentally fell into the cesspit and drowned.

As news of the boy's death spread, many people became out-raged by the injustice of the boy's fate. One such affected person said, "You tell us now, how is goodwill rewarded? How can we say that karma exists in this world? This boy made a living by sell-ing baked wheat cakes, and he was doing quite well for himself. But then he had to try to make some merit: first he gets fired and becomes a beggar, and then he contracts scabies and goes blind! Finally, after he settles down in the temple, he falls into the cesspit and drowns! How can you say that goodwill is rewarded?"

This kind of talk spread throughout the community until it reached the ears of the old monk. One day the old monk had gath-ered all the villagers together for a teaching, and used the opportu-nity to explain the fate of the boy:

"According to that boy's karma, he would have suffered for three lifetimes: During the first lifetime he was to be poor and de-velop scabies; during the second lifetime he was to go completely blind; and during the third lifetime he was to fall into a latrine and drown. However, due to his one compassionate thought to give and generate great merit, the negative karmic effects of three lifetimes were combined into one, sparing him the hardship and torment of the two other lifetimes. Now he has already been re-born in heaven!"

With his one thought of compassion and his act of giving, the boy who sold baked wheat cakes eliminated the negative karma of three lifetimes all at once.

The people who were outraged at the injustice of the boy's fate were treating the Dharma and merit like a business transac-tion, but sometimes what we only see with our physical eyes is not how things truly are. How things look on the surface are but a temporary combination of conditions; a false appearance created by the deluded mind. If we allow our minds to abide in deluded thoughts and deluded notions, we will alternate between faith and doubt, and then it will be impossible to attain enlightenment. This is why the *Diamond Sutra* says of itself that we should "believe it and not turn our minds against it." Only when we are not alarmed, not frightened, and not scared can our bodies and minds be free. Then the mind need not abide in anything.

<16> "Subhuti, good men and good women during the period of declining Dharma will receive, uphold, read, and chant this sutra. If their virtues were completely described, there are some who would go mad upon hearing it, and they would form deep doubts and not believe it. Subhuti, you should know that the teachings of this sutra are inconceivable, and its karmic results are inconceivable."

The Buddha states here that the meanings of the *Diamond Sutra* are so profound that they cannot even be conceived of, and that no language can fully describe them. The positive karmic results that can be attained through receiving and upholding the sutra are also inconceivable, for they are limitless and incalculable. The great master Sengzhao once said:

> All the merit from this teaching transcends the mind, hence it cannot be imagined by the mind; it transcends language, hence it cannot be explained verbally. It cannot be weighed with a scale or quantified by any measure. If a person realizes the emptiness of self and phenomena and deeply understands true reality through this sutra, then

their merit will be vast and on par with that of the Buddha mind, which is limitless and incalculable.

The Firm Mind Is Like a Diamond

In the time of the Buddha there lived a ruthless murderer who harmed countless people because of his misguided belief that killing people and taking their finger-bones would enable him to ascend to heaven and attain liberation. After killing someone, he would take one of their finger bones and string it onto a garland of many finger bones that he wore around his neck. People were terrified of him and abhorred his grisly cruelty. The people called him Angulimala, Sanskrit for "finger-garlanded heretic."

Later the Buddha encountered Angulimala and, because of the Buddha's transformative teachings, he ordained as a Buddhist monk and began to live a wholesome life. However, when he entered the city to gather alms with the other monastics, the city's residents had still not forgotten the evil deeds he had committed, so they threw dirt and stones at him, and would curse and defame him. Each day Angulimala would always end up with his clothes soiled and torn and his faced bruised and streaked with blood.

One day, the Buddha called for Angulimala and consoled him compassionately, "Angulimala, you must remain composed and unshakable, and find joy in receiving the teachings. As you continue to practice in accordance with the Dharma so assiduously, your previous negative karma will be like salty, foul water poured into a great quantity of pure water, such that in time it, too, will be refreshing and drinkable. The Dharma is like moonlight breaking through the layers of clouds to illuminate your mind, ensuring that you follow the correct path. The seeds of negative karma you sowed in the past must be repaid with pure, wholesome karma, so that when the clouds of darkness disperse, you will see moonlight shining everywhere, illuminating yourself and others."

Due to his faith and understanding of the Buddha's teachings, the mind of the murderous Angulimala became like the great earth itself, immovable and unshakeable, as he transformed himself from the murderous "finger-garlanded heretic" into an arhat.

"Furthermore, Subhuti, if those good men and good women who receive, uphold, read, and chant this sutra are disdained by others, it is due to negative karma incurred in a former life. That negative karma should be the cause of the person falling into a lower realm, but in this life, he is merely disdained. Eventually his negative karma from previous lives will be eradicated, and he will attain *anuttara samyaksambodhi*."

In the above passage the Buddha says to Subhuti that if someone single-mindedly practices, upholds, reads, and chants the *Diamond Sutra* and does not garner the respect of human and heavenly beings, but is instead cursed or despised by others, this is because such people have extremely grave negative karma from previous lives. Such karma should lead them to fall into the three lower realms and suffer there, but if they are able to patiently endure and maintain their practice even as they are despised by others, then the purity of their faith can make their past karma slowly disappear. In the future they will realize unsurpassed, perfect enlightenment.

The English variant *karma* is derived from the Sanskrit term *karman*, meaning "action," and refers to physical and mental actions, deeds, and intentions. Karma is generally divided into three categories: physical karma, verbal karma, and mental karma. Karma is also divided into positive karma, negative karma, and neutral karma (which is neither positive nor negative). If the karma created is of the five great violations[4] or ten unwholesome actions,[5] then one will surely suffer the negative karmic effect of rebirth in the three lower realms of the animal realm, the realm of hungry ghosts, and the hell realm. If one generates the positive karma of the five precepts and the ten wholesome actions, then in future one may experience rebirth in the human or heavenly realm.

The karmic obstacles we encounter can be formed either from the karma of past lives or the karma of our current lives, but all such obstructions serve to obscure the intrinsic nature of suchness so that we continue to travel through the cycle of birth and death in the six realms of existence. As we receive, uphold, read, and recite the *Diamond Sutra*, we will come to realize the wondrous wisdom of *prajna* and understand that everything is illusory and fabricated. Rather than being altered by circumstances or driven by karma, such understanding allows us to alter our own circumstances. By delving deep into *prajna* we completely purify false fabrications and remove karmic obstacles.

Before Chan Master Fayuan Yuanjian was enlightened, he and Chan Master Tianyi Yihuai had heard of the great wisdom of Chan Master Guixing in Ye County, so they decided to travel there and request the teachings. It was winter and bitterly cold, with a heavy snow blowing in the wind. Eight monastics in total made the journey to Guixing's place. As soon as he saw them, Chan Master

---

4. Killing one's father, killing one's mother, killing an arhat, shedding the blood of a Buddha, and creating a schism in the sangha. *Ed.*

5. Killing, stealing, sexual misconduct, lying, duplicitous speech, harsh speech, flattery, greed, anger, and ignorance. *Ed.*

Guixing loudly scolded them and tried to drive them away, but the group was unwilling to leave. Guixing then threw water on them, soaking their clothing and bedding. The six other members of the group could not bear this, and so they left in disgust. Fayuan and Yihuai simply straightened their robes and knelt on the ground, begging not to be sent away.

Shortly thereafter, Chan Master Guixing scolded them once more, "So you won't leave? Is it that you're waiting for me to beat you with a stick?"

Fayuan replied earnestly, "The two of us have traveled hundreds of miles to come and study here. How can a ladle of water possibly send us away? Even if you beat us with clubs, we still will not leave."

Chan Master Guixing replied, "Since you really came here to learn, go and register for lodgings."

Upon registering with the receptionist, Fayuan served for a time as monastery cook. On one occasion he took some oil and noodles without asking and made some five-flavored porridge to offer to the monastic community. After Chan Master Guixing found out about this, he reprimanded Fayuan with extremely harsh words: "You have misappropriated temple property and made an offering to the monastic community on your own. Besides corporeal punishment in accordance with the monastery rules, you must pay back the monastery for the cost of the goods."

Chan Master Guixing then gave Fayuan thirty strokes with the meditation stick. The value of Fayuan's robe, bowl, and sitting mat were assessed to repay the value of the food, so they were taken as payment and Fayuan was driven out of the temple.

Even after being driven out of the temple gate, Fayuan was still unwilling to leave, and instead would sleep standing up each night in the hallway of the dormitory. After Chan Master Guixing learned of this, he again rebuked Fayuan saying, "This hallway belongs to the monastery, and is to be used only by members of our monastic community. Why are you staying here? The rent you owe to the monastery will be calculated and billed to you."

After Fayuan was told how much he owed the monastery, he displayed no sense of reluctance whatsoever, but went to the marketplace and began to chant sutras in hope of receiving donations to pay back what he owed.

Not long after, Chan Master Guixing spoke to all the monastics at the monastery and said, "Fayuan is a true Chan practitioner, and a vessel for the Dharma."

He then had a servant invite Fayuan into the assembly hall, and in front of all those gathered there, presented Fayuan with the Dharma robe and gave him the name Chan Master Yuanjian, meaning "perfect mirror."

Offering the Three Karmas

The six *paramitas* are what transform our afflictions into enlightenment. Among the six, the *paramita* of patience is sure to be tested while we cultivate the spiritual path. However, the most difficult trials offer the greatest and most enduring blessings. One concrete example of such a series of trials to learn the Dharma is the life of Milarepa.

Milarepa's hometown was located in the Gungtang Province[6] of Posterior Tibet. While his parents lived, Milarepa's entire family supported themselves from the lands bequeathed by his grandfather, allowing them quite an affluent lifestyle.

---

6. Located north of present-day Gyirong county in Western Tibet near the Ngari region. *Ed.*

When Milarepa was seven, his father died, and in his will he clearly stipulated that Milarepa was to inherent the entire estate upon reaching adulthood. The will also requested that his paternal aunt and uncle were to act as his guardians. However, not only did his aunt and uncle take over the estate, they even forced Milarepa and his mother to labor endlessly in the fields during the blazing heat of the summer months. Over time, the villagers grew to despise Milarepa and his mother. Milarepa's mother swallowed her sadness and put up with the ill-treatment until Milarepa came of age. Once Milarepa became an adult, the aunt and uncle then simply sent both mother and son away. Milarepa's mother was full of rage and resentment, and she had Milarepa swear an oath that he would take his revenge on these wicked foes.

Milarepa then went to Ü-Tsang, a province in western Tibet, and began to study sorcery, quickly mastering it. He cast a spell which killed thirty-five people, including his uncle's son, daughter-in-law, family members, and friends. Fearing that people in the village may seek revenge, his mother sent word that Milarepa would summon a hailstorm to destroy the grain seedlings to intimidate the villagers into not taking action. And so Milarepa sent another hailstorm that destroyed the crops of the entire village. However, Milarepa was kind and good by nature, and felt great remorse over what he had done, so he decided to dedicate the rest of his life to seeking liberation through practicing the Dharma as a disciple of the Buddhist teacher Marpa.

Marpa tested Milarepa in a hundred different ways. First he said to Milarepa, "Construct a stone building for storing Buddhist texts. After that is done I will transmit the Dharma to you."

Milarepa had finished construction on half of the building when Marpa said to him, "I didn't think this out clearly beforehand.

This is not the right place. You should go to the top of the western mountain and build it there."

All Milarepa could do was tear down what he had built, stone by stone and beam by beam, and then carry these materials over to the western mountain for construction there. Milarepa was about halfway through when Marpa spoke once more, "That's all wrong! You should go build it on top of the northern mountain. And it should be shaped like a triangle."

Milarepa's rebuilding was about a third of the way completed when Marpa spoke up yet again:

"This looks like an altar for practicing sorcery. Tear it down!"

Having built up and then torn down the structure several times, Milrepa's back was already very worn and bruised, and he was enduring an unbearable level of pain. But his teacher demanded that he construct a nine-story building in the shape of a cube. Milarepa worked quickly day and night, and Marpa's three main disciples even helped him to move stones. When Marpa found out, he had Milarepa tear out any stones that others had moved into place. He said that each and every stone and wooden beam must be put in place by Milarepa personally.

After the construction of the building was finished, Marpa angrily drove Milarepa away and said, "Is that your offering? Do you think that constructing this building makes you so great?"

As he continued to try to make a suitable offering to his teacher, Milarepa solicited donations by wandering with his alms bowl, garnering enough to purchase a large, square copper lamp. He then offered the lamp to his teacher in hopes that Marpa would teach him the Dharma and pass onto him his secret teachings as soon as possible. Instead, Marpa ordered Milarepa to call down a hailstorm upon the two villages of Yehpo and Yemo. After finishing this task,

Milarepa requested the teachings once again. Marpa surprised Milarepa, and told him, "Only when you restore the crops belonging to the villages of Yehpo and Yemo, will I transmit the Dharma to you!"

Milarepa was ashamed. The fact that he could not receive the Dharma pained him greatly, and he was sad and hopeless. Marpa's wife consoled Milarepa with tears in her eyes. She stole Marpa's ruby seal along with some jewelry that belonged to Naropa, Marpa's teacher, and gave them to Milarepa. She also forged a letter which would enable Milarepa to gain an audience with Marpa's chief disciple, Lama Ngokpa. When Ngokpa saw the letter, he immediately bestowed upon Milarepa the empowerment and secret instructions pertaining to the deity Hevajra. Even then, without Marpa certifying his transmission, Milarepa couldn't connect with the teachings no matter how assiduously he practiced.

Before long, Marpa ordered Ngokpa and Milarepa to come and see him. Marpa thundered with rage, and scolded both his wife and Ngokpa. Marpa then said, "In order to eliminate Milarepa's past negative karma, I tested him in a hundred different ways so that he must practice austerity. Over the course of the past eight phases in austere practice, his karmic hindrances have mostly been eliminated. I will now give him my blessing and bestow upon him the empowerments and instructions, enabling him to succeed in his practice."

Those present were so happy for Milarepa that many were moved to tears.

The story of Milarepa shows us that Buddhahood is to be realized by human beings. Everyone can attain Buddhhood as long as there is determination, renunciation, and forbearance. In the end, Milarepa's genuine devotion to his teacher and his assiduous and diligent cultivation of the practice was able to eliminate his severely negative karma and attain enlightenment.

Just after the *Diamond Sutra* opens, it is said that Subhuti "rose from his seat, bore his right shoulder, knelt on his right knee, and [pressed his palms] together before him"—this is how to make an offering to the Buddha with purity of body, speech, and mind, and respectfully request that the Buddha teach the Dharma. The *Diamond Sutra* begins with daily life, for the best kind of practice is to offer the three kinds of karma every day:

1. Offer physical karma by doing good deeds.
2. Offer verbal karma by speaking good words.
3. Offer mental karma by keeping good thoughts.

Everywhere Is a Temple

Even an ordinary person can become as solid as a diamond as long as they are able to eliminate their delusions and attachments and believe in their own Buddha nature, their ability to become enlightened, and their own unlimited potential. The *Lankavatara Sutra* says, "Consider the amala fruit; it ripens gradually." In learning Buddhism one cannot act rashly. An amala fruit does not go from bud to fruit all at once, but rather ripens bit by bit. All the flowers, grasses, and trees of the earth grow gradually, and there is no way to force them to grow faster. All human learning, even artistic pursuits like singing, dancing, calligraphy, and painting are all perfected gradually.

As referenced before there is an old Buddhist saying: "Without a meditation breakthrough, do not dwell in the mountains. Without meditative insight, do not go on retreat." This means that, after some major breakthrough, one can go off into the mountains to practice what was learned. After a moment of insight, one may be able to confirm it more fully on retreat. There are some people who want to rush off and live in a mountain hermitage as soon as they first encounter Buddhism. But even if we understand enlightenment in theory, it still takes a lot of hard work to truly be enlightened. No one can grow up and mature all at once. In Buddhism sometimes we talk about "sudden enlightenment" versus "gradual enlightenment"—both approaches are fine, and both require time. Once one has perfected one's merit and created the proper conditions, success will come naturally. Cultivation is not assuming some style or putting on an act, it should develop naturally, for only in that way can it be true reality as it is.

One day, the king of Zhao made a special effort to visit Chan Master Zhaozhou Congshen. At the time, Congshen was lying down resting in bed and he said to the King of Zhao, "Oh great king, I've grown old. I know you have made this trip expressly to see me, but I do not have the strength to get out of bed and receive you. Please do not take offense."

The king of Zhao was not offended at all, but rather was overjoyed, and the two talked together quite happily. Once the king of Zhao returned, he sent one of his generals to deliver a series of gifts to the Chan master. When the general arrived with the gifts, Congshen got out of bed at once and greeted the visitor at the door.

Congshen's disciples were confused. One disciple asked, "When the king of Zhao came yesterday, you would not get out of bed. But when his subordinate came today, why did you get out of bed to greet him?"

Chan Master Congshen replied, "There's something you don't understand. My way of receiving guests is as follows: For first-class guests, I lie in bed and greet them using my intrinsic nature. For second-class guests, I go to the guest hall and treat them courteously. For third-class guests, I go to the front gate to greet them respectfully in accordance with good social form."

The story of Chan Master Congshen's manner of greeting guests became well known. Centuries later the great Song dynasty poet Su Shi was preparing to visit Chan Master Foyin at Jinshan Temple, and he wrote to him beforehand requesting that they dispense with all the complicated greeting ceremonies, just as Chan Master Congshen received the king of Zhao.

When Su Shi arrived at Jinshan Temple, he saw Chan Master Foyin standing outside the temple's main gate to greet him. Su Shi felt quite satisfied with himself and said, "Why is it that you can't let go of worldly social conventions? It seems to me that your practice cannot compare with the free-spirited unconventionality of Chan Master Zhaozhou Congshen, as I see you came all the way out here to receive me."

Su Shi thought that he would render the Chan master speechless, but Foyin waved his palm leaf fan, and leisurely spoke the following verse:

> Zhaozhou, on that day, was less than humble,
> Not coming out of the monastery gate
> to receive the king of Zhao.
> You do not know the immeasurable form
> of Mount Jin
> The great universe is my Chan bed.

Su Shi clung to the physical appearance of receiving guests. Chan Master Foyin had no such attachments to physical appearances, and could regard the entire universe as his Chan bed. When the entire universe is your bed, how is it possible to distinguish between being in bed and getting out of bed? This is having a mind that does not abide in anything. Being excessive or overly restrained are both attachment. Clinging to the five desires and the six sense objects is, of course, insatiable, but we can also go too far in seeking an otherworldly life such that we appear lonely and dejected. By cultivating meditative concentration and wisdom together we can harmonize the worldly and the transcendent. In fact, one of the principles of Humanistic Buddhism is to use what transcends this world to do worldly work.

The famous poet Tao Qian once said, "I build my cottage in the world of men / Yet there is no clamor of horse and carriage." One of the insights that the Sixth Patriarch Huineng gained from the *Diamond Sutra* that he shares in the *Platform Sutra* is that existence and non-existence are not dualistic, and to understand such is to live a life of non-thought and non-discrimination. This way, every place can become like a temple for enlightenment. In a similar fashion, we should use the transcendent qualities of Buddhism, such as vast, limitless compassion, and apply it to the work of liberating living beings.

Perfected Humanity Is Perfected Buddhahood

26 If anyone should think that I can be seen among forms,
Or that I can be sought among sounds,
Then that person is on the wrong path
And he will not see the Tathagata.

As mentioned previously, *tathagata* or *rulai* (如來) in Chinese is one of the epithets of the Buddha. The true nature of the Tathagata is unshakable, and it pervades all of the dharma realm. When the Tathagata comes, he has not truly come, and though sometimes he is hidden away, when he goes he has not truly gone. Because he does not come or go, he is called Tathagata, "thus come."

In the above, "coming" and "going" can refer to the relative distinctions between things, but how is it that the Tathagata, who has realized and attained the Dharmakaya, does not manifest it? In the *Diamond Sutra* it says that, "'Tathagata' means all phenomena as they are." The Tathagata is one who realizes the principle of "suchness": that absolute and immovable reality which pervades as many worlds as there are grains of sand in the Ganges River and extends throughout the three thousand-fold world system. That is another way in which the Tathagata "does not come from anywhere and does not go anywhere."

The Treatise on the Awakening of Faith in Mahayana states:

> The intrinsic essence of suchness neither increases nor decreases in ordinary people, *sravakas*, *pratyekabuddhas*, bodhisattvas, or all Buddhas. It does not arise in the beginning nor does it cease in the end and is absolutely eternal. From the very beginning, suchness by its very nature is perfectly endowed with all meritorious qualities. Namely, its essence is endowed with the quality of the light of great wisdom; the quality of illuminating the dharma realm; the quality of real cognition; the quality of mind in its intrinsic purity; the qualities of permanence, bliss, purity, an independent

self, unchangeableness, and freedom. It possesses inconceivable teachings more numerous than the grains of sand along the Ganges River, from which it is not separated, disconnected, nor made different. And as it is perfect and lacks in nothing whatsoever, it is called the *tathagatagarbha*, and it is also called the Tathagata Dharmakaya.

The term "Tathagata" also suggests adapting the teachings to conventional truth, which are taught in order to liberate living beings through skillful means. If someone believes that the Buddha is without the notion of self, others, sentient beings, or longevity, then how can the Buddha say of himself that he had attained Buddhahood, become a Dharma king, and is free and unobstructed by all phenomena? "Tathagata" is the true self of the Dharmakaya. In his coming and going, his sitting and lying down, the Buddha was acting in accordance with worldly appearances. The Buddha realized the fruit of enlightenment but did not abide in the appearance of Buddhahood.

Once there was a temple abbot who had been reciting the name of Amitabha Buddha for more than twenty years. Since he began practicing, he had always hoped that he would see Amitabha Buddha with his own eyes so that he could confirm his practice. Finally one night he had a dream in which a bodhisattva from Amitabha Buddha's Western Pure Land of Ultimate Bliss said to him, "Your devotion to Amitabha Buddha surpasses most. I have been sent by Amitabha Buddha to tell you that tomorrow he will come to visit you in person."

After he awoke, the abbot recited the name of Amitabha Buddha with even more joyous devotion. He sat in front of the

Buddha hall with the name of Amitabha Buddha always on his lips, as he patiently waited to welcome the arrival of Amitabha Buddha. The abbot waited all day, the sun slipped behind the mountains, and Amitabha Buddha never appeared. He began to doubt: Was it really possible that Amitabha Buddha did not keep his word?

That night, the bodhisattva appeared in his dream again. Just as the abbot was preparing to complain about how Amitabha Buddha did not keep his word, the bodhisattva spoke, "What is wrong with you? Amitabha Buddha came to see you three times yesterday, yet you were unwilling to receive him."

The abbot replied, "But no one told me that Amitabha Buddha had arrived!"

The bodhisattva said, "You must be blind. Amitabha Buddha first came early in the morning as a begging woman. He had just reached your door when you told a servant to chase her away. Around noon Amitabha Buddha came again as a householder woman. When she reached the main shrine you didn't look at her even once, and when she told your servant to announce her visit to you, the servant said that you never receive female guests. In the evening, Amitabha Buddha manifested as a stray dog, but as soon as the dog entered the gate the receptionist scared him off with a stick!"

The abbot replied, "I had no idea that was Amitabha Buddha."

 "Subhuti, what do you think? Can the Buddha be seen as his physical body, complete [with the thirty-two marks of excellence and eighty noble characteristics]?"

"No, World-honored One, the Buddha should not be seen as his physical body. And why is this? The Tathagata has said that his complete physical body is not the complete physical body, and that this is what is called the complete physical body."

"Subhuti, what do you think? Can the Tathagata, complete in all forms, be seen or not?"

"No, World-honored One, the Tathagata should not be seen as complete in all forms. And why is this? The Tathagata has said that complete in all forms is not complete and that that is what is called complete in all forms."

In the passage quoted above, the Buddha is addressing ordinary people who become fixated on physical appearance and try to understand the Buddha in terms of how he looks or sounds. The Buddha is said to possess "thirty-two marks of excellence and eighty noble characteristics" which describe his voice and appearance, but these two are simply temporary manifestations which arise from causes and conditions for the sake of liberating living beings. As the proper causes and conditions come together they appear, and when the conditions are no longer present they disappear. They are nothing more than temporary manifestations that exist at a certain time. This cannot be the Tathagata's eternal Dharmakaya that does not come or go.

"Subhuti, never say that the Tathagata has the thought, 'I have spoken the Dharma'. Do not have that thought. And why is this? If someone says that the Tathagata has spoken the Dharma, then that person is defaming the Buddha, and he does not understand what I have been

> saying. Subhuti, when a person speaks the Dharma no
> Dharma can be spoken, and thus it is called speaking the
> Dharma."

The Buddha spoke the Dharma as conditions arose and did not cling to the notion of the Dharma. The way that Tathagata teaches is by manifesting as the one who speaks the Dharma. In every case he adapts his teachings in accordance with the spiritual capacity of the audience and manifests a physical form where there previously was no form, and manifests speech where there was once no speech. Saying that the Tathagata "speaks the Dharma" is a worldly notion; that is why Subhuti is told that someone who thinks that the Tathagata "has spoken the Dharma" is defaming the Buddha.

All that the Buddha says is said for the sake of unlocking the intrinsic nature of suchness that living beings inherently possess. The Buddha speaks as conditions arise to eliminate the delusions of living beings, liberating them in accordance with their spiritual capacities.

So what then is the Dharma? In the *Diamond Sutra*, the Buddha also says, "...my teachings should be understood to be like a raft.[7] If even the Dharma must be let go of, what about that which is not the Dharma?" We should get rid of the notion of "Dharma" and "non-Dharma" so that a thought like "the Buddha has spoken the Dharma" does not arise to abide in.

Once a certain Buddhist monk came to see Chan Master Dazhu Huihai and said, "I would like to ask a question. Can you answer it?"

Dazhu said, "The moon reflected in the deep pool can be pondered as one wishes."

---

7. This is a reference to a famous parable of the Buddha's. The Dharma is like a raft in that, once it is used to cross the river of life and death, it should be left at the shore rather than carried on land. *Ed.*

The monk then asked, "What is the Buddha?"

Dazhu replied, "If it is not the Buddha across from the clear pool, then who?"

Everyone gathered there was confused when they heard this. Finally, the monk spoke up, "May I ask you, great master, what Dharma you teach to liberate people?"

Dazhu said, "I don't have a single teaching that can liberate people."

The monk said, "You Chan masters always speak of wonder and emptiness."

Dazhu then offered a counter question, "What Dharma do you, virtuous one, speak to liberate people?"

The monk answered, "I teach the Diamond Sutra."

Dazhu then asked, "Who speaks this sutra?"

The Buddhist monk angrily retorted, "Now you're just trying to make fun of me. Everyone knows it is a sutra spoken by the Buddha."

Dazhu then proceeded to quote the sutra: "'If someone says that the Tathagata has spoken the Dharma, then that person is defaming the Buddha, and he does not understand what I have been saying.' yet if someone says that this sutra was not spoken by the Buddha, then that person has defamed the sutra. Please explain, virtuous one."

The monk was completely stumped.

By saying that he did not have a single teaching that could liberate people, Chan Master Dazhu Huihai showed a deep understanding of the Buddha's meaning in the *Diamond Sutra*. All the sutras of all the Buddhas do nothing more than wipe away the dust of delusion that obscures our ordinary mind, allowing us to see the intrinsic nature of *prajna*. The Buddha repeatedly enjoined those practitioners who aspire to unsurpassed, perfect enlightenment to empty themselves of any notion concerning living beings, the form of the Buddha, the form in which the Buddha speaks the Dharma, and other such notions. The Buddha wishes us to be free and undisturbed, and to return to the inherent mind.

In the *Lotus Sutra* it is said that Aksayamati Bodhisattva once asked the Buddha, "How did Avalokitesvara Bodhisattva come to this Saha World? How does he teach the Dharma for the sake of living beings? How does he apply the power of skillful means?"

The Buddha then answered, "Good man, if there are living beings in this land who should be liberated by someone in the form of a Buddha, then Avalokitesvara Bodhisattva will manifest in the form of a Buddha and teach the Dharma to them."

When someone hears this part of the Buddha's teaching, he may wonder: Avalokitesvara is a bodhisattva, which is defined as one who has not yet attained Buddhahood. How can a bodhisattva manifest in the form of a Buddha to teach living beings? Is that not masquerading as the Buddha?

Many people may have questions like this, but the answer is that, no, this is not the same as impersonating the Buddha. Avalokitesvara has actually already attained Buddhahood long, long ago, and was named Zhengfa Ming Tathagata (正法明如來), "Clearly Understanding the True Dharma." However, after he attained Buddhahood he did not forget about living beings, and thus returned to the Saha World where beings live in torment. Here he conceals his Buddhahood and manifests in the form of a bodhisattva to give compassionate aid to living beings.

An arhat is one who dedicates a small amount of merit to many, while Avalokitesvara Bodhisattva dedicates great merit to a few. Avalokitesvara Bodhisattva compassionately stepped back from assuming a Buddha's form so that he could guide and liberate all those who suffer, so that they may realize the six *paramitas* and attain the tranquility of *nirvana*.

That being said, even though Avalokitesvara Bodhisattva has stepped back out of compassion, dedicates great merit to a few, and conceals his Buddhahood by appearing as a bodhisattva, he actually possesses all the practices, vows, and conduct of the Buddhas. This is how Avalokitesvara Bodhisattva is able to manifest as a Buddha to teach the Dharma; it is not deception. Additionally, the bodhisattva manifests as a Buddha only for a given time when there is a person who can be liberated by the form of a Buddha. Avalokitesvara Bodhisattva then manifests the form of a Buddha only for a period of time as a skillful means to instruct and guide living beings.

Since Avalokitesvara Bodhisattva has already attained Buddhahood, he is capable of billions upon billions of manifestations, which he uses to spread the Dharma and liberate living beings. No matter what kind of sentient beings, as long as they possess the capacity to understand, the bodhisattva will explain the Dharma to them so that they can transform their ignorance into enlightenment. This is what is meant by the expression "there is no standard Dharma." There is no standard Dharma, just as there is no standard physical appearance of the Buddha, and we should not become attached to either.

Enlightenment does not lie in being able to recite a thousand Buddhist verses and cannot be found by browsing through the Buddhist sutras. Enlightenment lies in how we use the mind in our daily lives and in every thought. We must not dismiss the minutia of life, for even boiling water to make tea or carrying rocks and firewood all contain the causes and conditions for attaining enlightenment. This is why the *Diamond Sutra* opens with a description of the Buddha's simple monastic lifestyle. This shows that genuine cultivation is not a performance or a show, and we should never be concerned with making some pretentious or esoteric display, or trying to one-up each other. The Buddha maintained a simple daily routine and simple food and dress so that he could live free and at ease with a perfectly dignified manner. This allows those with only a tenuous commitment to practice to have faith that, if they put forth the proper effort, they too can be like the Buddha.

I have spent my entire life honoring the Buddha and learning from him, but I do not wish to become a Buddha or a Buddhist patriarch. I am generous and do good deeds, but I do not want to go to heaven. I recite Amitabha Buddha's name, but I have no desire to gain rebirth in the Pure Land. My aim is not to transcend life and death, but rather to cultivate more resources for Buddhism. I wish to be reborn as an ordinary monk in the human world lifetime after lifetime.

In the *Samyukta Agama*, the Buddha wants Ananda to answer how he would explain if non-Buddhist monks were to ask the Buddha why he teaches celibacy. At one time, the Buddha was in the city of Sravasti at the Jeta Grove Monastery teaching the Dharma, and he asked Ananda, "Supposing there was a non-Buddhist monk who came to you and asked, 'Ananda, why does the Buddha teach his disciples to be celibate?' How would you answer him?"

Ananda replied, "Lord Buddha, I would tell them in accordance with your teachings that we practice in this way to renounce form, so that attraction does not arise in the mind. When one is able to turn away from desire he can proceed to eliminate all afflictions until he attains liberation and realizes the state of tranquility, emptiness of the mind, and the universal nature of the Dharma, which does not arise or cease. After having turned away from physical form, we practice with the remaining four aggregates of feeling, perception, mental formations, and consciousness. One who is no longer bound by the five aggregates can connect to the Buddha mind. Lord Buddha, if non-Buddhist monks were to ask me such a question, I would answer them in this way."

The Buddha said, "Well done, Ananda, well done! You should answer the question in this way. And why is that? I definitely teach celibacy so that people may practice the renunciation of form, turn away from desire, eliminate all affliction, and attain liberation."

In the *Mahaparinirvana Sutra*, the Buddha further tells Ananda, "Lay a mat for me between two trees in such a way that my head points north and my face looks to the west. Why? In the future the Dharma will spread and advance far north."

Ananda answered, "Yes," and laid out the mat at once.

At that moment, all the deities who lived in those trees caused the trees to bloom out of season, and they scattered their flowers on the ground. The Buddha told Ananda, "The deities living in these two trees have made an offering of these flowers, which are blooming out of season. However, this is not the way to make offerings to the Buddha."

Ananda asked, "How then should one make an offering to the Buddha?"

The Buddha replied, "If one is able to receive the Dharma and practice it, then enlightenment is used as a flower offering. Only in this way can one make real offerings to the Buddha."

At that time, Ananda said to the Buddha, "While the Buddha is in the world, the monastics from all directions, the elder monastics, and the practitioners with deep understanding of the teachings and the monastic rules have all come to see the Buddha. We disciples make use of such opportunities to pay homage to and learn from them. But they will not come after the Buddha's final *nirvana*, and we will lose what all these good Dharma friends could teach us."

The Buddha replied, "You should not despair. All you need to do is constantly remember the four kinds of mindfulness. The first is to be mindful of the place the Buddha was born, the second is to be mindful of the place of the Buddha's enlightenment, the third is to be mindful of the place the Buddha turned the Dharma wheel, and the fourth is to be mindful of the place of the Buddha's final *nirvana*. Ananda, all good men and women who receive and uphold what the Buddha has taught should be mindful of the place the Buddha was born and remember the Buddha's virtue of practicing the Dharma over many *kalpas*; be mindful of the place of the Buddha's enlightenment and remember the Buddha's virtue of subduing the armies of Mara; be mindful of the place the Buddha turned the Dharma wheel and remember the Buddha's virtue of compassion to broadly liberate sentient beings; and be mindful of the place of the Buddha's final *nirvana* and remember the Buddha's virtue of his unshakably peaceful tranquility. Anyone who upholds these four mindfulnesses and four virtues will not be separated from the Buddha and good Dharma friends, day or night.

"Ananda, do you think you will have no protection and will lose your support after the Buddha's *nirvana*? Do not think this way. All the teachings and precepts I have given since I attained Buddhahood will be your protection and your support. The Buddha's teachings will become a Dharma vessel that allows living beings in the period of the declining Dharma to sail over to the shore of liberation and serve as protection and support for timid bodies and minds. For those who can put the Buddha's final teachings into practice, it will be as if the Buddha is still in the world."

Why do sentient beings suffer? Why are they not enlightened? Because of affliction and attachment. As soon as we form attachments we cannot attain liberation, as our afflictions become inexhaustible. But where do these attachments come from? Attachments are produced by a mind that is ignorant and selfish. We must not become attached to what we hope to attain, for what we know is so limited, and attachment just makes that limited knowledge even more rigid and narrow. If we can get rid of our selfishness and our deluded attachments we can eliminate our afflictions. With no afflictions we can attain enlightenment and liberation, and experience the perfection of *nirvana* in the human world.

A jet airplane can fly at the speed of sound through the use of turbojet engines. The way that a turbojet engine works is by sucking air into a compressor, the air is pressurized and enters a combustion chamber where it is mixed with fuel and burned, which then immediately flows through the turbine, causing the turbine to spin at high velocity. Finally, the high temperature and high velocity exhaust jets out the nozzle. It is this reaction that supplies the powerful force of propulsion.

Isn't human life like this? If one can bear it, then high pressure and blazing fire can be transformed into a propelling force for progress. Difficulties and trials can become the gateways to success, and our thinking can transform difficulties into positives. Buddhism has many sayings that refer to this phenomenon, such as "the blaze of flames can become red lotuses" and "affliction is enlightenment." When we live our lives with determination and diligence anything is possible.

We do need both success and liberation in this life, it is only that it is impossible to achieve either of these by looking outwardly. Rather, one must come to recognize the truth that all phenomena are empty: Emptiness includes both existence and non-existence; emptiness is causes and conditions, for only true emptiness allows for all of wondrous existence. We should all go and directly investigate our own minds and find our own *prajna* wisdom. The mind of *prajna* is solid as a diamond, able to break through defilement and sorrow. Practicing the Dharma makes me feel happy, enriched, and blessed. Nothing is lacking. Everything happens naturally, and success simply occurs when the causes and conditions are right.

It is difficult to be born as a human being, and the Dharma, too, is not easy to encounter. Given that in this life we have obtained this human body and have the opportunity to hear the Dharma, our causes and conditions must be really special.

Humanistic Buddhism is Mahayana Buddhism and the Buddhism of the bodhisattva path that brings happiness and well-being to people. It is a Buddhism that advocates cultivation without attainment, and seeks to bring widespread success and universal liberation to living beings. When we make the Mahayana vow, we set our aspiration for enlightenment, the compassionate mind, and the development of skillful means. When we do so we can experience the mind-to-mind Dharma transmission of the Buddha through our intrinsically pure mind of *prajna*.

The *Platform Sutra* says: "Kindness and compassion is Avalokitesvara. Joy and equanimity is Mahasthamaprapta. The capacity for purity is Sakyamuni." These clearly show how important the mind of purity is.

I have been a Buddhist monastic for more than seventy years now, yet I have never spoken with the Buddha nor has a bodhisattva ever laid his hands upon my head to assure me of my future enlightenment. I have always been seeking, searching, and wondering: Where is the Buddha? Over the last few decades, I have gone to India on seven occasions to seek out the sacred sites related to the Buddha. I wandered over and looked around Lumbini Garden where the Buddha was born. I went to places like Uruvilva Forest, where the Buddha cultivated asceticism, and the Nairanjana River, where he bathed after renouncing his asceticism, hoping that I could see some traces of the Buddha. I bowed in homage to the Buddha's seat under the bodhi tree where he attained perfect enlightenment, hoping that the Buddha would appear to me. I circumambulated the teaching platform from which the Buddha turned the Dharma Wheel. And in particular, I bowed in homage at the sacred site near Kusinagara where the Buddha entered final *nirvana*. I could not bear leaving that place, for it seemed I was already drawing near the Buddha.

Later on, I felt that when eating, I was sharing the meal with the Buddha; when walking, the Buddha was guiding me. I arose in the morning with the Buddha, and went to bed each night holding the Buddha. I felt the Buddha in my heart, and knew that the Buddha is present wherever there is light, fresh air, and life. After all, the Buddha is the dharma realm and the universe itself.

There is a saying in Buddhism, "If you wish to know the state of the Buddha, you must make your thoughts as pure as empty space." If you can enlarge your mind to encompass space itself, then you will know what the Buddha is like. As Buddhists, we must realize our everlasting wisdom and let our lives flow into the universe, where we can be together with the Buddha and become one with space itself.

The Buddha is part of the human world, and so are we. What is the secret to success and fulfillment? It is to be found in the unrestrained and limitless potential of the mind of *prajna*. Single-mindedly thinking of the Buddha and single-mindedly acting like the Buddha combines knowledge and action into one, just like the two wings of a bird or the two wheels of a cart. Whether you are a monastic or a layperson, worldly or transcendent, the *Diamond Sutra* is a sutra that we can all receive with conviction and conscientiously put into practice in a flexible and practical manner.

The great Tang dynasty poet Li Bo once wrote: "People today cannot see the moon of ancient times / But the moon tonight once shone upon the ancients." There is no such thing as "modern" or "ancient" when it comes to the Dharma; enlightenment is in the moment! By universally bestowing the Dharma through skillful means, the Buddha was teaching wondrous applications of the *Diamond Sutra* to Subhuti and the other twelve hundred and fifty people assembled there. And since the Buddha is not bound by time or space, he is teaching us, as well.

Consider again the expression "Pervade across the ten directions and extend down through the three time periods." The expression "extend down through the three times periods" means to transcend the past, present, and future, while "pervade across the ten directions" is to transcend space, just as Amitabha Buddha is transcendent with infinite life and infinite light. Humanistic Buddhism is what we apply in daily life. We must transcend time in how we treat others and deal with our affairs. We cannot think about one time only, for yesterday, today, and tomorrow all exist in this instant and must be well looked after. Then there are the various conditions of one's relationships with the older, younger, and one's own generation, all of which must be well looked after. If you are unable to pervade across the ten directions when managing some enterprise, you will find that you offend your superiors and create difficulties for your subordinates. When we first encounter the Dharma, it may seem deep and profound, but when we apply it to our life the Dharma is simply what makes everything wonderful.

It is my wish that all people will become awakened to, live, and realize a life of freedom that does not abide in anything, and that together we can find fulfillment in this world, and achieve great success.

Appendix I

The Diamond Sutra

1

The Causes of This Dharma Meeting

Thus have I heard. At one time, the Buddha was in the city of Sravasti at the Jeta Grove Monastery with a gathering of monks numbering 1,250. At mealtime, the World-honored One put on his robe, picked up his bowl, and went into the city of Sravasti to beg for food. After he had gone from house to house, he returned to the grove. When he had finished eating, he put away his robe and bowl, washed his feet, straightened his mat, and sat down.

2

Subhuti's Request

At that time the elder monk Subhuti was among the gathering of monks. He rose from his seat, bore his right shoulder, knelt on his right knee, and with palms pressed together before him, respectfully spoke to the Buddha saying, "Rare, World-honored One, the Tathagata protects and is concerned about all bodhisattvas, and he instructs all bodhisattvas. World-honored One, when good men and good women commit themselves to *anuttara samyaksambodhi*, in what should they abide in, and how should they subdue their minds?"

The Buddha said, "Wonderful! Wonderful! Subhuti, it is as you have said, the Tathagata protects and is concerned about all bodhisattvas, and instructs all bodhisattvas. Now listen carefully while I tell you, when good men and good women commit themselves to *anuttara samyaksambodhi*, in what they should abide in, and how they should subdue their minds."

"Excellent, World-honored One. I will joyfully listen to what you say."

3

The Heart of the Mahayana

The Buddha said to Subhuti, "All great bodhisattvas should subdue their minds in the following manner: Of all sentient beings, be they born of eggs, wombs, moisture, or transformation, or whether they have form, or no form, or whether they are able to perceive, or do not perceive, or are neither able to perceive nor not perceive, I cause them to enter *nirvana* without remainder, liberating them. Thus by liberating infinite, immeasurable, limitless sentient beings, in reality, no sentient beings are liberated.

"And why is this? Subhuti, if a bodhisattva has the notion of a self, the notion of others, the notion of sentient beings, or the notion of longevity, then he is not a bodhisattva."

4

The Wonder of Behaving Without Attachment

"Moreover, Subhuti, within this phenomenal world, a bodhisattva should practice giving without abiding in anything. This means that he should not give abiding in form, nor should he give abiding in sound, smell, taste, touch, or *dharmas*. Subhuti, a bodhisattva should not give abiding in any notion whatsoever. And why is this? If a bodhisattva gives without abiding in any notion whatsoever, then his merit will be immeasurable.

"Subhuti, what do you think, can the vastness of space to the east be measured?"

"No, it cannot, World-honored One."

"Subhuti, can the vastness of space to the south, west, north, up, or down be measured?"

"No, it cannot, World-honored One."

"Subhuti, when a bodhisattva gives without abiding in any notion, his merit is just as immeasurable. Subhuti, a bodhisattva should abide in this teaching and this teaching alone."

5

Seeing the Truth That Lies Beneath Perception

"Subhuti, what do you think, can you see the Tathagata from his physical form?"

"No, World-honored One, no one can see the Tathagata from his physical form. And why is this? The Tathagata has said that physical form is not physical form."

The Buddha said to Subhuti, "All forms are illusory. If you see that all forms are not forms, then you see the Tathagata."

6

The Rarity of True Belief

Subhuti said to the Buddha, "World-honored One, can sentient beings, upon hearing these words, truly believe them?"

The Buddha told Subhuti, "Do not talk like that. Even after I have entered *nirvana* for five hundred years, there will still be people who uphold the precepts and generate merit who will believe these words and accept them as truth. You should know that they planted good roots not just with one Buddha, or two Buddhas, or three, or four, or five Buddhas, but that they planted good roots with infinite tens of millions of Buddhas. For a person who has one thought of pure belief, Subhuti, the Tathagata fully knows and fully sees that those sentient beings will attain such limitless merit. Such a person already does not have the notion of a self, the notion of others, the notion of sentient beings, the notion of longevity, the notion of phenomena, or the notion of non-phenomena.

"And why is this? If a sentient being clings to a notion with his mind, then he will cling to self, others, sentient beings, and longevity. If he clings to the notion of phenomena, then he will cling to self, others, sentient beings, and longevity. And why is this? If he clings to the notion of non-phenomena then he will cling to self, others, sentient beings, and longevity. Thus, he must not cling to phenomena or non-phenomena. This is why I have often said to you, *bhiksus*, that even my teachings should be understood to be like a raft. If even the Dharma must be let go of, what about what is not the Dharma?"

7

Nothing Had Been Attained and Nothing Has Been Said

"Subhuti, what do you think? Has the Tathagata really attained *anuttara samyaksambodhi*? Has the Tathagata really spoken the Dharma?"

Subhuti said, "As far as I understand what the Buddha has said, there is no standard Dharma that can be called *anuttara samyaksambodhi*, and there is no standard Dharma spoken by the Tathagata. And why is this? The Dharma of which the Tathagata speaks cannot be held on to, it cannot be spoken, it is not a phenomenon, and it is not a non-phenomenon. Why? All saints and sages are distinguished by their different understanding of the unconditioned Dharma."

8

Enlightenment Comes from These Teachings

"Subhuti, what do you think? If someone were to fill the three thousand-fold world system with the seven treasures, used them for giving, and attained merit for this, would the merit be great?"

Subhuti said, "It would be very great, World-honored One. And why is this? Such merit is not the nature of merit; thus the Tathagata says it is great."

"If someone else were to receive and uphold as few as four lines of verse from this sutra, and if he were to explain them to others, his merit would be even greater than that. And why is this? Subhuti, all Buddhas and all the supremely enlightened teachings of the Buddhas are born of this sutra. Subhuti, that which is called the Buddhadharma is not the Buddhadharma."

9

The Four Fruits Are Empty

"Subhuti, what do you think? Would it be right for a *srotapana* to think like this: 'I have attained the fruit of *srotapana*'?"

Subhuti said, "No, World-honored One. And why is this? *Srotapana* means 'stream-enterer', and yet there is nothing to be entered. To not enter into form, sound, smell, taste, touch, or *dharmas* is what is called *srotapana*."

"Subhuti, what do you think? Would it be right for a *sakradagami* to think like this: 'I have attained the fruit of *sakradagami*'?"

Subhuti said, "No, World-honored One. And why is this? *Sakradagami* means 'once-returner', and yet in truth there is no such thing as returning. This is what is called *sakradagami*."

"Subhuti, what do you think? Would it be right for an *anagami* to think like this: 'I have attained the fruit of *anagami*'?"

Subhuti said, "No, World-honored One. And why is this? *Anagami* means 'non-returner', and yet in truth there is no such thing as never returning. This is the reason it is called *anagami*."

"Subhuti, what do you think? Would it be right for an *arhat* to think like this: 'I have attained the path of an *arhat*'?"

Subhuti said, "No, World-honored One. And why is this? There is no phenomenon called 'arhat'. World-honored One, if an *arhat* were to think 'I have attained the path of an *arhat*', then he would be clinging to self, others, sentient beings, and longevity.

"World-honored One, the Buddha has said that I have attained passionless *samadhi,* and that among all people, I am the best in this; and that among all *arhats,* I am also the best at going beyond desire. And yet, I do not have the thought that I am a passionless *arhat.* World-honored One, if I were to have the thought that I had attained the path of an *arhat,* then the World-honored One would not have said that Subhuti takes delight in the practice of calm and quiet, free from temptations and distress. Subhuti, in reality, is without practice, and thus it is called delighting in the practice of calm and quiet."

10

Adorning the Buddha Land

The Buddha said to Subhuti, "What do you think? In the past, when the Tathagata was with Dipamkara Buddha, did he attain the Dharma?"

"No, World-honored One, when the Tathagata was with Dipamkara Buddha, he truly did not attain the Dharma."

"Subhuti, what do you say? Does a bodhisattva adorn the Buddha land?"

"No, World-honored One. And why is this? That which adorns the Buddha land is non-adornment, that is what is called adornment."

"For this reason, Subhuti, all great bodhisattvas should give rise to purity of mind in this way: they should not give rise to a mind that abides in form; they should not give rise to a mind that abides in sound, smell, taste, touch, or *dharmas*. They should give rise to a mind that does not abide in anything.

"Subhuti, what do you think? If a man's body were as large as Mount Sumeru, would that body be large?"

Subhuti said, "Very large, World-honored One. And why is this? The Buddha has said that it is not the real body, and thus is called a large body."

11

The Unconditioned Is Supreme

"Subhuti, if each grain of sand in the Ganges River were to become a Ganges River, and if the sand in all of those rivers were added up, what do you think? Would that be a lot of sand?"

Subhuti said, "It would be very much, World-honored One. The number of Ganges Rivers alone would be enormous; the amount of sand would be even greater than that."

"Subhuti, I will now truthfully tell you: if a good man or a good woman were to give away as many three thousand-fold world systems filled with the seven treasures as there are those grains of sand, would his merit be great?"

Subhuti said, "It would be very great, World-honored One."

The Buddha said to Subhuti, "If a good man or a good woman receives and upholds as few as four lines of verse from this sutra, and if he explains them to others, then his merit will be greater."

12

Honoring the True Teaching

"Furthermore, Subhuti, anyone who explains this sutra, even four lines of verse from it, should be honored by people in this world, by those in heaven, and by *asuras* as if he were a Buddhist shrine. What then of anyone who receives, upholds, reads, and chants the teachings of this sutra with all of his strength? Subhuti, you should know that such a person already has become accomplished in the highest and rarest Dharma. Wherever this sutra can be found, there also is the Buddha; and it should be honored as if it were one of his disciples."

13

The Name of This Sutra

At that time, Subhuti asked the Buddha, "World-honored One, what should this sutra be called, and how should we receive it and uphold it?"

The Buddha said to Subhuti, "This sutra is called the *Diamond Prajnaparamita*, and by this name you should receive it and uphold it. And why is this? Subhuti, the Buddha has said that *prajnaparamita* is not *prajnaparamita* and that that is what is called *prajnaparamita*. Subhuti, what do you think? Does the Tathagata speak the Dharma?"

Subhuti said to the Buddha, "World-honored One, the Tathagata has not said anything."

"Subhuti, what do you think? Is all the fine dust throughout the three thousand-fold world system a lot of dust or not?"

Subhuti said, "It is a lot, World-honored One."

"Subhuti, the Tathagata says that all of that fine dust is not fine dust, and that that is what is called fine dust. The Tathagata says that the world is not the world, and that that is what is called the world. Subhuti, what do you think? Can the Tathagata be seen by his thirty-two marks?"

"No, World-honored One. And why is this? The Tathagata has said that the thirty-two marks are not marks, and that that is what is called thirty-two marks."

"Subhuti, suppose a good man or good woman were to give his or her own life as many times as there are grains of sand in the Ganges, if one were to receive and uphold even four verses of this sutra and explain it to others, his merit would be greater."

14

Ultimate Tranquility Beyond Notions

Then, after hearing this sutra and comprehending its deep meaning, Subhuti wept out loud and said to the Buddha, "Rare, World-honored One, the Buddha has spoken such a deep, profound sutra. Since obtaining the wisdom eye I have not heard such a sutra. World-honored One, if anyone should hear this sutra and believe it with a pure mind, then he will give rise to true reality. You should know that this person will attain the supreme, rarest virtue. World-honored One, true reality is not reality, and that is what the Tathagata calls true reality.

"World-honored One, today I have heard this sutra, believed it, understood it, received it, and upheld it, and this was not difficult. If five hundred years from now, someone should hear this sutra, believe it, understand it, receive it, and uphold it, then that person will be a rare person indeed. And why is this? That person is without a notion of self, notion of others, notion of sentient beings, or notion of longevity. And why is this? The notion of a self is not a notion, and the notion of others, sentient beings, and longevity are not notions. And why is this? That which turns away from all notions is called all Buddhas."

The Buddha said to Subhuti, "So it is, so it is. Moreover, if a person hears this sutra and does not become alarmed, or frightened, or scared, then this person is indeed a rare person. And why is this? Subhuti, the Tathagata has said that the supreme *paramita* is not the supreme *paramita*, and that this is what is called the supreme *paramita*. Subhuti, the Tathagata has said that the *paramita* of patience is not the *paramita* of patience. And why is this? Subhuti, long ago when my body was being cut apart by King Kalinga, I had no notion of self, no notion of others, no notion of sentient beings, and no notion of longevity. And why was this? If at that distant time, as my body was being cut apart piece by piece, if I had had a notion of self, a notion of others, a notion of sentient beings, or a notion of longevity, I would have become angry. Subhuti, think about this some more; five hundred lifetimes ago when I was a practitioner of patience, I was without a notion of self, a notion of others, a notion of sentient beings, or a notion of longevity. For this reason, Subhuti, a bodhisattva should turn away from all notions, and initiate the mind of *anuttara samyaksambodhi*. He should not give rise to a mind abiding in form, and he should not give rise to a mind abiding in sound, smell, taste, touch, or *dharmas*. He should give rise to a mind that does not abide in anything. If the mind abides in anything it is a false abiding. Thus, the Buddha says that a bodhisattva should not give abiding in form. Subhuti, a bodhisattva should give in this way to benefit all sentient beings. The Tathagata says that all notions are not notions, and therefore he also says that all sentient beings are not sentient beings.

"Subhuti, the Tathagata is a speaker of what is true, what is real, what is so, what is not deceptive, and what is not altered. Subhuti, the Dharma that the Tathagata has attained is not real and it is not unreal.

"Subhuti, when the mind of a bodhisattva abides in phenomena and practices giving he is like a person who has entered into darkness—he sees nothing at all. When the mind of a bodhisattva does not abide in any phenomena and practices giving, he is like someone who has eyes in the full light of the sun—he sees all forms clearly.

"Subhuti, if in future lifetimes there are good men and good women who can receive, uphold, read, and chant this sutra, the Tathagata fully knows and fully sees that these people will attain infinite, limitless virtue."

15

The Merit of Upholding This Sutra

"Subhuti, suppose a good man or good woman were to give as many of his or her lives as there are grains of sand in the Ganges River in the morning, and give as many of his or her lives as there are grains of sand in the Ganges River at noon, and give as many of his or her lives as there are grains of sand in the Ganges River in the afternoon, and that this giving continued for infinite hundreds of millions of billions of kalpas; if someone were to hear this sutra, believe it, and not turn his mind against it, his merit would be greater—what of the merit of one who copies, receives, upholds, reads, chants, and explains it to others?

"Subhuti, in summation, the virtue of this sutra is infinite and unlimited. The Tathagata speaks this sutra to those who have initiated the mind of the the Great Vehicle; he speaks it to those who have initiated the mind of the Supreme Vehicle. For those who receive, uphold, read, chant, and explain this sutra to others, the Tathagata fully knows and fully sees that such people will attain infinite, immeasurable, limitless, inconceivable virtue. All such people will shoulder the *anuttara samyaksambodhi* of the Tathagata. And why is this? Subhuti, those who delight in the lesser Dharma cling to a view of self, a view of others, a view of sentient beings, and a view of longevity, and thus they are not able to listen to this sutra, to receive it, to read it, to chant it, or to explain it to others.

"Subhuti, in whatever place this sutra can be found, all who are in the world should make offerings to it, as should all in heaven, and all *asuras.* They should treat this place as if it were a pagoda; they should surround it, bow to it, and pay their deepest respect to it. They should scatter incense and flowers all around this place."

16

Purification of Karma

"Furthermore, Subhuti, if those good men and good women who receive, uphold, read, and chant this sutra are disdained by others, it is due to negative karma incurred in a former life. That negative karma should be the cause of the person falling into a lower realm, but in this life he is merely disdained. Eventually his negative karma from previous lives will be eradicated, and he will attain *anuttara samyaksambodhi.*

"Subhuti, I remember infinite *asamkhya kalpas*, ago, when I was before Dipamkara Buddha, I met, honored, and made offerings to all of the eighty-four hundred billion *nayutas*[1] of Buddhas in the universe without excluding a single one of them. If someone during the period of declining Dharma can recieve, uphold, read, and chant this sutra, the virtue he will attain will be a hundred times—nay, a million, billion times, nay, an incalculable number of times that cannot even be suggested by metaphors—greater than the virtue I attained for honoring all Buddhas.

"Subhuti, good men and good women during the period of declining Dharma will receive, uphold, read, and chant this sutra. If their virtues were completely described there are some who would go mad upon hearing it, and they would form deep doubts and not believe it. Subhuti, you should know that the teachings of this sutra are inconceivable, and its karmic results are inconceivable."

17

Complete and Utter Selflessness

Then Subhuti asked the Buddha, "World-honored One, when good men and good women initiate the mind to *anuttara samyaksambodhi*, what should they abide in? And how should they subdue their minds?"

The Buddha said to Subhuti, "When good men and good women initiate the mind to *anuttara samyaksambodhi*, they should give rise to a mind like this: 'I should liberate all sentient beings, and as I liberate them, I should know that there really are no sentient

---

1. A nayuta is an extremely large number, usually calculated to equal one hundred billion. *Ed.*

beings to be liberated.' And why is this? If a bodhisattva has a notion of self, notion of others, notion of sentient beings, or notion of longevity, then he is not a bodhisattva. And why is this? Subhuti, in truth, there is no phenomenon of initiating the mind to *anuttara samyaksambodhi*.

"Subhuti, what do you think? When the Tathagata was with Dipamkara Buddha, was there the Dharma of *anuttara samyaksambodhi* to attain or not?"

"There was not, World-honored One. As far as I understand the meaning of what the Buddha has said, when the Buddha was with Dipamkara Buddha, there was no Dharma of *anuttara samyaksambodhi* to attain."

The Buddha said, "So it is, so it is. Subhuti, in truth, there is no Dharma of *anuttara samyaksambodhi* for the Tathagata to attain. Subhuti, if the Tathagata had attained the Dharma of *anuttara samyaksambodhi*, then Dipamkara Buddha would not have prophesized, 'In the future you will attain Buddhahood and be called Sakyamuni.' Since there is no Dharma of *anuttara samyaksambodhi* to attain, Dipamkara Buddha prophesized that I would become a Buddha, saying, 'In the future you will attain Buddhahood and be called Sakyamuni.' And why is this? 'Tathagata' means all phenomena as they are. Someone might say, 'The Tathagata has attained *anuttara samyaksambodhi*,' but Subhuti, there really is no Dharma of *anuttara samyaksambodhi* for the Buddha to attain. Subhuti, within the *anuttara samyaksambodhi* that the Tathagata has attained there is no real nor unreal.

"For these reasons, the Tathagata says that all phenomena are the Buddhadharma. Subhuti, that which is said to be all phenomena is not all phenomena, and that is why it is called all phenomena. Subhuti, it is the same as a great human body."

Subhuti said, "World-honored One, the Tathagata has said that a great human body is not a great human body, and that that is why it is called a great human body."

"Subhuti, a bodhisattva is just like that, and if he should say, 'I should liberate all sentient beings', then he is not a bodhisattva. And why is this? Subhuti, in reality there is no phenomenon called 'bodhisattva', and for this reason the Buddha has said that all phenomena are without self, without others, without sentient beings, and without longevity. Subhuti, if a bodhisattva should say, 'I adorn the Buddha land,' then he is not a bodhisattva. And why is this? The Tathagata has said that that which adorns the Buddha land is non-adornment, and that that is what is called adornment. Subhuti, only after a bodhisattva has fully understood no self and no phenomena will the Tathagata say that he is a true bodhisattva."

18

One Body Sees All

"Subhuti, what do you think, does the Tathagata have eyes of flesh or not?"

"Yes, World-honored One, the Tathagata has eyes of flesh."

"Subhuti, what do you think, does the Tathagata have heavenly eyes or not?"

"Yes, World-honored One, the Tathagata has heavenly eyes."

"Subhuti, what do you think, does the Tathagata have wisdom eyes or not?"

"Yes, World-honored One, the Tathagata has wisdom eyes."

"Subhuti, what do you think, does the Tathagata have Dharma eyes or not?"

"Yes, World-honored One, the Tathagata has Dharma eyes."

"Subhuti, what do you think, does the Tathagata have Buddha eyes or not?"

"Yes, World-honored One, the Tathagata has Buddha eyes."

"Subhuti, what do you think, has the Buddha said that the sand in the Ganges River is sand or not?"

"Yes, World-honored One, the Tathagata has said that it is sand."

"Subhuti, what do you think, if there were as many Ganges Rivers as there are grains of sand in the Ganges River, and if all of the sand in all of those rivers were added up, and if the number of Buddha worlds equaled the number of all of those grains of sand, would that be a lot?"

"It would be very much, World-honored One."

The Buddha said to Subhuti, "The Tathagata fully knows and fully sees the minds of the sentient beings in all of these worlds. And how can this be? The Tathagata has said that all minds are not minds and that thus they are called minds. And why is this so? Subhuti, the mind of the past cannot be obtained, the mind of the present cannot be obtained, and the mind of the future cannot be obtained."

19

Universal Transformation Within the Dharma Realm

"Subhuti, what do you think? If someone were to fill the three thousand-fold world system with the seven treasures, and used them for giving, with this as a cause and condition, would he attain immense merit?"

"So it is, World-honored One. With this as a cause and condition he will attain immense merit."

"Subhuti, if there really were such a thing as merit, the Tathagata would never speak about attaining immense merit. It is only because there is no such thing as merit that the Tathagata says that immense merit can be attained."

20

Beyond Form and Notions

"Subhuti, what do you think? Can the Buddha be seen as his physical body, complete [with the thirty-two marks of excellence and eighty noble characteristics]?"

"No, World-honored One, the Buddha should not be seen as his physical body. And why is this? The Tathagata has said that his complete physical body is not the complete physical body, and that this is what is called the complete physical body."

"Subhuti, what do you think? Can the Tathagata, complete in all forms, be seen or not?"

"No, World-honored One, the Tathagata should not be seen as complete in all forms. And why is this? The Tathagata has said that complete in all forms is not complete and that that is what is called complete in all forms."

21

Speaking the Unspeakable

"Subhuti, never say that the Tathagata has the thought, 'I have spoken the Dharma'. Do not have that thought. And why is this? If someone says that the Tathagata has spoken the Dharma, then that person is defaming the Buddha, and he does not understand what I have been saying. Subhuti, when a person speaks the Dharma no Dharma can be spoken, and thus it is called speaking the Dharma."

Then the wise Subhuti said to the Buddha, "World-honored One, will there ever be sentient beings in the future who, upon hearing this teaching, will believe it?"

The Buddha said, "Subhuti, those sentient beings are not sentient beings, and they are not not sentient beings. And why is this? Subhuti, the Tathagata has said that all sentient beings are not sentient beings, and that this is what is called sentient beings."

22

The Unattainable Dharma

Subhuti said to the Buddha, "World-honored One, the Buddha attained *anuttara samyaksambodhi*, yet nothing was attained?"

"So it is, so it is, there is not even the slightest Dharma that can be attained in *anuttara samyaksambodhi*, and this is what is called *anuttara samyaksambodhi*."

23

Perfect Equanimity

"Furthermore, Subhuti, the Dharma is equal and without high or low. This is called *anuttara samyaksambodhi*. Because one is without self, without others, without sentient beings, and without longevity, he practices all wholesome teachings and attains *anuttara samyaksambodhi*. Subhuti, what is called 'all wholesome teachings,' the Tathagata says are not all wholesome teachings, and thus they are called all wholesome teachings."

24

True Generosity Lies in Upholding This Sutra

"Subhuti, suppose a person give a quantity of the seven treasures equal to all the Sumeru mountains within a three thousand-fold world system; if another person were to use this *prajnaparamita* sutra, even as few as four lines of verse, and receive, uphold, read, chant, and explain it to other, his merit would be one hundred times— nay, a hundred million, billion times, nay, an incalculable number of times that cannot even be suggested by metaphors—greater."

25

Transforming That Which Cannot Be Transformed

"Subhuti, what do you think? Do not say that the Tathagata has this thought: 'I should liberate sentient beings'. Subhuti, do not have this thought. And why is this? In reality, there are no sentient beings for the Tathagata to liberate. If there were sentient beings for the Tathagata to liberate, then the Tathagata would have a notion of self, others, sentient beings, and longevity.

"Subhuti, when the Tathagata speaks of a self, it is the same as no self, and yet all ordinary people take it as a self. Subhuti, the Tathagata says that ordinary people are not ordinary people, and that this is what is called ordinary people."

26

The Dharma Body Is Without Notion

"Subhuti, what do you think? Can the Tathagata be seen by his thirty-two marks or not?"

Subhuti said, "So it is, so it is. The Tathagata can be seen by his thirty-two marks."

The Buddha said, "Subhuti, if the Tathagata could be seen by his thirty-two marks, then a wheel turning monarch would be the same as the Tathagata."

Subhuti said to the Buddha, "World-honored One, as far as I understand the meaning of what the Buddha has said, one should not to be able to see the Tathagata by his thirty-two marks."

> If anyone should think that I can be seen
>   among forms,
> Or that I can be sought among sounds,
> Then that person is on the wrong path
> And he will not see the Tathagata.

27

Nothing Is Ended and Nothing Is Extinguished

"Subhuti, suppose you had this thought: 'It is not because his marks are complete that the Tathagata attains *anuttara samyaksambodhi*.' Subhuti, do not have this thought, 'It is not because his marks are complete that the Tathagata attains *anuttara samyaksambodhi*'.

"Subhuti, suppose you had this thought: 'Those who initiate the mind of *anuttara samyaksambodhi* advocate the Dharma of annihilation.' Do not have this thought. And why is this? Those who initiate the mind of *anuttara samyaksambodhi*, in regards to the Dharma, do not advocate the annihilation of notions."

28

Not Receiving and Not Wanting to Receive

"Subhuti, suppose a bodhisattva gave a quantity of the seven treasures capable of filling as many worlds as there are grains of sand in the Ganges River; if a bodhisattva knows that all phenomena are without self and thereby attains patience the virtue he attains is superior. Subhuti, this is because all bodhisattvas do not receive this merit."

Subhuti said to the Buddha, "World-honored One, why is it that bodhisattvas do not receive merit?"

"Subhuti, the merit of a bodhisattva should not be attached to. That is why it is said that they do not receive merit."

29

Awesome Tranquility

"Subhuti, if someone says, '["Tathagata" means] "thus come," does he come? Does he go? Does he sit? Does he lie down?' then this person has not understood my meaning. And why is this? The Tathagata has not come from anywhere, and he is not going anywhere, and that is why he is called the Tathagata."

30

Compound Notions

"Subhuti, if a good man or a good woman were to pulverize a three thousand-fold world system into fine dust, what do you think, would that collection of fine dust be a lot or not?"

"It would be a lot, World-honored One. And why is this? If that collection of fine dust were something that really existed, the Buddha would not have called it a collection of fine dust. And why is this? The Buddha has said that a collection of fine dust is not a collection of fine dust and so it is called a collection of fine dust. World-honored One, the three thousand-fold world system the Tathagata has spoken about is not a three thousand-fold world system and that is what is called a three thousand-fold world system. And why is this? If that world really existed, then it would be a unified form. The Tathagata has said that a unified form is not a unified form, and so it is called a unified form.

"Subhuti, that which is a unified form cannot really be spoken about, and yet ordinary people are attached to it."

31

Not Giving Rise to Belief in Notions

"Subhuti, if a person were to say, 'The Tathagata teaches a view of self, a view of others, a view of sentient beings, and a view of longevity', Subhuti, what do you think, has this person understood the meaning of what I am saying?"

"No, World-honored One. This person has not understood the meaning of what the Tathagata is saying. And why is this? The World-honored One has said that a view of self, a view of others, a view of sentient beings, and a view of longevity is not a view of self, a view of others, a view of sentient beings, and a view of longevity, and so it is called a view of self, a view of others, a view of sentient beings, and a view of longevity."

"Subhuti, one who initiates the mind of *anuttara samyak-sambodhi* should not give rise to the notion of phenomena. He should know all phenomena in this way; he should know and view them like this, and believe and understand them like this. Subhuti, the Tathagata says that that which is called a notion of phenomena is not a notion of phenomena, and so it is called a notion of phenomena."

32

Like Shadows, Like Bubbles, Like Dreams

"Subhuti, suppose a person were to give a quantity of the seven treasures capable of filling infinite *asamkhya* worlds, if a good man or good woman were to initiate the bodhisattva mind and use this sutra, even as few as four lines of verse from it, and were to receive, uphold, read, chant, and explain it to others, his merit is greater. And how should this sutra be taught to people? By not grasping to notions and being unmoved by things as they are. And why is this?"

> All conditioned phenomena
> Are like dreams, illusions, bubbles, and shadows,
> Like dew and lightning.
> One should contemplate them in this way.

When the Buddha finished speaking this sutra, the elder Subhuti, along with all the *bhiksus, bhiksunis, upasaka, upasika, asuras*, and worldly and celestial beings, heard what the Buddha had said, and all of them were greatly pleased, and they all believed it, received it, and practiced it.

Appendix II

Verses of the Diamond Sutra

In ancient Indian literature, the verse form was often used to offer praise or tribute, and the most common type of verse was the four-line stanza. The four-line verse has since become one of the standard Buddhist poetic forms.

In the *Diamond Sutra* the four-line verse is mentioned several times as a small unit of the *Diamond Sutra* to compare practicing even a small part of the sutra as exceeding other grandiose acts of merit. This shows the importance of the four-line verse in the sutra, such that some of its most impactful moments are presented in this form. For example, one particularly notable verse is found in chapter thirty-two:

> All conditioned phenomena
> Are like dreams, illusions, bubbles, and shadows,
> Like dew and like lightning;
> One should contemplate them in this way.

The essence of the Buddha's forty-nine years of teaching are contained within these four lines. All phenomena appear in the world as a combination of causes and conditions that is temporary by nature. When faced with any given phenomena, a moment of social interaction between oneself and others, or any current praise or blame, success or failure; if any of these abide in the mind then one can easily develop painful affliction and create all manner of distinctions and comparisons. Unhappiness in the past can plant the seed for scheming and prejudice, while even having positive or successful conditions in the present can set the stage for future worries and complaints when things do not work out as we hoped. How can the mind be purified?

The Buddha said that we should give rise to a mind that does not abide in anything. Similarly he says in the *Diamond Sutra* that, "The mind of the past cannot be obtained; the mind of the present cannot be obtained; and the mind of the future cannot be obtained." In the *Platform Sutra*, Huineng says, "Within each thought, do not revisit past states. If past, present, and future thoughts are linked together thought by thought as a continuum, this is called being bound. When thought after thought does not abide in any phenomena, that is called being unbound."

We must do our best in the moment, yet what is past is past. No matter thought we abide in, we become bound by affliction and a continuity of thought is formed. Only when the mind does not abide in anything can we be truly pure and free.

The "four notions" mentioned throughout the sutra, the notion of self, the notion of others, the notion of sentient beings, and the notion of longevity all arise from the notion of self. When we cling to our various desires we create a distinction between ourselves and others which gives rise to such notions. The notion of self arises as a result of the inability to control the five aggregates of form, feeling, perception, mental formations, and consciousness due to their conditional, illusory existence. Once we let go of the attachment to the notion of self, the three other notions will become undone accordingly. "Non-self" is *prajna*. In this instance too we must use the transcendental to practice what is worldly, and borrow from our worldly sense of self to practice towards non-self. Only when there is no self, no distinction, no true or false, no suffering, and no obstructions can the self manifest as true *prajna*.

Seeing the Buddha

> If anyone should think
>   that I can be seen among forms,
> Or that I can be sought among sounds,
> Then that person is on the wrong path
> And he will not see the Tathagata.

This four-line verse from chapter twenty-six shows how the pure Dharmakaya of the Buddha does not have an appearance. When we look for the Buddha, we should look for the true Dharmakaya, rather than becoming attached to the form or sound of the Buddha.

Once there was a Korean monk named Gyeongman who was known for his high moral principles. One night, he brought back to his room a woman with shoulder-length hair, and the two did not come out for several days. His disciples were baffled and, after a few more days, they could not bear it any longer and burst into their teacher's chamber. What they saw was their teacher sitting on the side of the bed, giving the woman a massage.

One of the disciples spoke up and said, "Master, how can behavior like this serve as an example for us?"

"Why can't it serve as an example for you?" the teacher replied.

The disciple pointed at the woman and stammered, "Don't you see? Don't you see?"

Gyeongman replied, "Come and look. Come and look."

The group of disciples drew in to take a closer look and saw that the woman had no nose, and her ears were gone as well, while her eyes were sunken in. She was a leper, and their teacher was in the process of giving her a special treatment. Gyeongman had kept her from everyone else because her illness was contagious. At that moment the disciple who had questioned his teacher knelt down in shame and said, "Master, only you are capable of such kindness."

What we see with our own eyes is never completely true, nor is what we hear with our ears. We must learn to do without our eyes, ears, nose, tongue, body, and mind. We must dispense with distinctions in order to realize in our own lives the real reason we are here, and the true mind, for only then can there be *prajna*. As the Buddha said, "If anyone should think that I can be seen among forms, or that I can be sought among sounds," then that is not the Buddha.

How then can we see the Buddha? When we see the workings of dependent origination, we see the Dharma, and so too do we see the Buddha. When we see *prajna* we see the Buddha. When we witness unconditional loving-kindness and compassion, we see the Buddha. Have a universal and all-encompassing mind, and you too will see the Buddha.

List of Texts

Venerable Master Hsing Yun extensively quotes the Buddhist sutras throughout his teachings, often sharing short passages from a staggering variety of works. If a reader is moved by a particular passage, the next step of visiting the literature itself can be a difficult one. An alphabetical list of sutras is provided below to assist in this process. The sutras are organized by their titles in English, except in such cases when the Sanskrit name of the text has become commonplace, as in the case of the *Dharmapada*. Each text is also listed with its common Chinese title, both in Chinese characters and pinyin pronunciation.

Combined Sources from the Five Lamps
  Wudeng Huiyuan   五燈會元

Diamond Sutra
  Jingang Jing   金剛經

Dirgha Agama
  Chang Ahan Jing   長阿含經

Ekottara Agama
  Zengyi Ahan Jing   增壹阿含經

Encouragement for Generating the Aspiration for Enlightenment
Quanfa Putixin Wen 勸發菩提心文

Exegesis on the Diamond Sutra
Jingang Jing Jieyi 金剛經解義

Flower Adornment Sutra
Huayan Jing 華嚴經

Heart Sutra
Xin Jing 心經

Lankavatara Sutra
Lengqie Jing 楞伽經

Lotus Sutra
Fahua Jing 法華經

Mahaparinirvana Sutra
Dabo Niepan Jing 大般涅槃經

Mind Seal Commentary to the Diamond Sutra
Jingang Bore Boluomi Jing Xinyin Shu 金剛般若波羅蜜經心印疏

Miscellaneous Treasures Sutra
Za Baozang Jing 雜寶藏經

Original Vows of Ksitigarbha Bodhisattva Sutra
Dizang Jing 地藏經

Perfection of Great Wisdom Sutra
  Mohe Bore Jing   摩訶般若經

Platform Sutra
  Liuzu Tan Jing   六祖壇經

Samyukta Agama
  Za Ahan Jing   雜阿含經

Suramgama Sutra
  Lengyan Jing   楞嚴經

Sutra in Forty-two Sections
  Sishier Zhang Jing   四十二章經

Sutra on the Causes and Conditions of King Surupa
  Miaose Wang Yinyuan Jing   妙色王因緣經

Treatise on the Awakening of Faith in Mahayana
  Dacheng Qixin Lun   大乘起信論

Treatise on the Middle Way
  Zhong Lun   中論

Treatise on the Perfection of Great Wisdom
  Dazhi Du Lun   大智度論

Upasaka Precepts Sutra
  Youpose Jiejing   優婆塞戒經

Vastly Profound and Gloriously Pure Non-Retrogressing Dharma Wheel Sutra
   Guangbo Yanjing Butui Zhuanlun Jing   廣博嚴淨不退轉輪經

Vimalakirti Sutra
   Weimo Jing   維摩經

List of Names

Provided below is a list of the important people mentioned in the text to assist readers interested in finding additional information in other sources. The names below are paired with the Chinese characters for the name, or for the most common Chinese transliteration of the name. Dates indicate the person's birth and death unless, otherwise noted, and all dates are given in the common era.

Name	Chinese	Date
Bailing	百靈	ca. 9th cent.
Baizhang Huaihai	百丈懷海	720-814
Bodhidharma	菩提達摩	d. 535
Caoshan Huixia	曹山慧霞	ca. 9th-10th cent.
Damei Fachang	大梅法常	752-839
Daoming	道明	780-877
Daoqian	道謙	d. 1155
Dazhu Huihai	大珠慧海	ca. 8th-9th cent.
Emperor Wu	梁武帝	502-549
Fayuan Yuanjian	法遠圓鑑	991-1067
Foyin	佛印	1032-1098
Fu Dashi	傅大士	497-569
Hongren	弘忍	602-675
Huanglong	黃龍	1002-1069
Huineng	慧能	638-713
Ikkyu	一休	1394-1481
Jinbifeng	金碧峰	ca. late 14th cent.

Koho Kennichi	佛國	1241-1316
Kumarajiva	鳩摩羅什	344-413
Li Mi'an	李密菴	ca. 17th-18th cent.
Longtan Chongxin	龍潭崇信	d. 838
Marpa	馬爾巴	1012-1097
Mazu Daoyi	馬祖道一	709-788
Milarepa	密勒日巴	1052-1135
Muso Soseki	夢窗疎石	1275-1351
Myoan Eisai	明菴榮西	1141-1215
Naropa	那諾巴	956-1041
Pang Yun	龐蘊	d. 808
Puwan	溥畹	ca. 17th-18th cent.
Seisetsu Shucho	誠拙	1745-1820
Sengzhao	僧肇	384-414
Su Manshu	蘇曼殊	1884-1918
Su Shi	蘇軾	1037-1101
Taigu Ryokan	大愚良寬	1758-1831
Tao Qian	陶潛	365-427
Tianhuang Daowu	天皇道悟	748-807
Tianran	天然	739-824
Tianyi Yihuai	天衣義懷	989-1060
Weishan Lingyou	溈山靈祐	771-853
Xiangyan Zhixian	香嚴智閑	d. 898
Xing'an	省庵	1686-1734
Xuanzang	玄奘	600-664
Yaoshan	藥山	751-834
Yishan	一山	1247-1317
Yunmen Wenyan	雲門文偃	864-949
Zhaozhou Congshen	趙州從諗	778-897
Zhizhe	智者	538-579

Glossary

Amitabha Buddha: The Buddha of boundless light and boundless life. Amitabha is one of the most popular Buddhas for devotion among Mahayana Buddhists. He presides over the Western Pure Land of Ultimate Bliss.

anuttara samyaksambhodi: A Sanskrit term meaning complete, unexcelled enlightenment; an attribute of all Buddhas.

Avalokitesvara Bodhisattva: The bodhisattva of compassion, whose name in Sanskrit means "Observing the sounds of the world." He is known as one of the great bodhisattvas of Mahayana Buddhism, and is very popular throughout China. The Universal Gate chapter of the *Lotus Sutra* features him prominently.

bodhi: (*Skt.* "awakening") Enlightenment. In the state of enlightenment, one is awakened to the true nature of self, that is, one is enlightened to one's own Buddha nature. Such a person has already eliminated all afflictions and delusions and has achieved *prajna*.

bodhisattva: While the term can describe a practitioner anywhere on the path to Buddhahood, it usually refers to a class of beings who stand on the very edge of full enlightenment, but remain in the world to help other beings become enlightened.

Buddha: (*Skt.* "awakened one") Though there are many Buddhas, the term typically refers to Sakyamuni Buddha—the historical Buddha, and founder of Buddhism.

Buddha nature: The capacity to become a Buddha that is inherent to all living beings.

causes and conditions: Commonly used to analyze causal relationships in a Buddhist context. In this form of analysis, a cause denotes the major factor which produces an effect. A condition is a factor which allows for a cause to produce a given effect. In the cause and effect phenomena of the growth of a plant, the seed is the cause, the sprouting of the seed is the effect, and factors such as the soil, sunlight, and water are the necessary conditions.

Chan (School): A school of Buddhism relying on meditative concentration for the path to liberation. "Chan" is also used to describe the aesthetic and way of life that developed out of this school.

dependent origination: The Buddhist concept that all phenomena arise due to causes and conditions. The central principle that phenomena do not come into existence independently but only as a result of causes and conditions; thus, no phenomena possesses an independent self-nature. This concept is also referred to as interdependence. The twelve factors of dependent origination are ignorance, mental formations, consciousness, name and form, the six sense organs, contact, feeling, craving, clinging, becoming, birth, and aging and death. The term is also sometimes used to specifically refer to the chain of causes that result in suffering, sickness, and death.

Dharma: (Skt. "truth.") Refers to the Buddha's teachings, as well as the truth of the universe. When capitalized, it means the ultimate truth and the teachings of the Buddha. When the Dharma is applied or practiced in life it is referred to as righteousness or virtue. When it appears with a lowercase *d*, it refers to anything that can be thought of, experienced, or named; close in meaning to "phenomena."

Dharmakaya: One of the three "bodies" of the Buddha. The Dharmakaya is the aspect of the Buddha that is present throughout all of existence.

dharma realm: The true nature of our world, as seen without defilement or affliction. May also refer to a cosmological scheme which includes the six realms of existence (*see* realm), plus the realms of *sravakas*, *pratyekabuddhas*, bodhisattvas, and Buddhas.

emptiness: A Buddhist doctrine that all phenomena have no essence or permanent aspect whatsoever. Consequently, everything that exists in the world is due to dependent origination and has no permanent self or substance. Emptiness can be basically categorized into two types: 1) emptiness of people (living beings), which means that human beings or other living beings have no unchanging, substantial self; and 2) emptiness of phenomena, which means that existence of all phenomena are due to causes and conditions.

enlightenment: The state of awakening to the truth of existence; freedom from all afflictions and sufferings.

five aggregates: The five aggregates make up a human being. They are form, feeling, perception, mental formation, and consciousness.

Fo Guang Shan: A monastery founded by Venerable Master Hsing Yun in 1967 in Kaohsiung, Taiwan. Fo Guang Shan is also the association of over two hundred branch temples around the world.

gongan: Also known in Japanese as *koan*. Literally "public notice" in Chinese that originally referred to a legal precedent. However, this became a term adopted by the Chan tradition to refer to a phrase, or question and answer exchange that points to an essential paradox. Contemplation of a *gongan* is aimed at transcending logical or conceptual assumptions in order to intuit the ultimate reality of emptiness.

hell: The lowest of the six realms of existence. There are many hell realms. In all of them suffering is so intense that little, or no, progress can be made toward enlightenment. Avici hell (*Skt.* "without reprieve") is said to be the longest of all the levels of suffering.

Humanistic Buddhism: Buddhism practiced in a way that is engaged with the world and life-affirming. Major tenets include the integration of Buddhism with life and the creation of a "pure land on Earth." Venerable Master Hsing Yun is a proponent of Humanistic Buddhism.

intrinsic nature: The fundamental essence of all living beings. (*see* Buddha nature)

Jambudvipa: The terrestrial world in Buddhist cosmology where human beings reside.

kalpa: An Indic unit of time measurement. A *kalpa* is an incalculably long period of time spanning the creation and destruction of the universe.

karma: Literally "action," though much more commonly used to describe the entirety of the Buddhist view of cause and effect. The Buddha stated that the causes, conditions, and rebirth that we encounter in the future are effects of our previous thoughts, words, and deeds.

Manjusri Bodhisattva: The bodhisattva of wisdom.

Mara: A malevolent being that embodies desire and is an adversary of the Buddha. The name is also used to refer to mental qualities that impede spiritual progress.

nirvana: A state of perfect tranquility that is the ultimate goal of Buddhist practice.

Noble Eightfold Path: The path leading to enlightenment taught by Sakyamuni Buddha. It includes right view, right thought, right speech, right action, right livelihood, right effort, right mindfulness, and right meditative concentration.

non-self: (*Skt. anatman*) A basic concept in Buddhism that says that all phenomena and beings in the world have no real, permanent, and substantial self. Everything arises, abides, changes, and extinguishes based on the law of dependent origination.

paramita: Sanskrit word meaning "to cross over," denoting passage to the other shore of the tranquility of nirvana. Spiritual success.

pratyekabuddha: One who attains enlightenment on his or her own, without having heard the teachings of a Buddha.

Pure Land: A transcendent realm created through the power of a Buddha's vow to help ease the suffering of living beings, should they choose to be reborn there.

realm: Used variously to describe several different Buddhist cosmological schemes. The "six realms of existence" refers to possible destinations of rebirth, and includes heaven, the *asura* realm, the human realm, the animal realm, the realm of hungry ghosts, and hell. The "three realms" includes the desire realm, the form realm, and the formless realm, and corresponds both to destinations of rebirth and meditative attainment.

sangha: The Buddhist community. In a broad sense it includes both monastics and laypeople, though most often it refers only to monastics.

six senses: The six senses of human beings are sight (*alt.* form), sound, smell, taste, touch, and dharmas (phenomena).

sravaka: Literally "one who has heard." A *sravaka* is one who has been liberated from the cycle of rebirth after listening to the Buddha's teachings, but does not seek to become a Buddha.

suchness: A term for the true nature of all things; the pure, original essence of all phenomena.

sutra: A Sanskrit word used to describe a variety of religious and non-religious writings, but most commonly used in a Buddhist context to refer to the recorded discourses of the Buddha.

Tathagata: One of the ten epithets of the Buddha. It means "thus come" and "thus gone."

three thousand-fold world system: The Buddhist cosmology containing an infinite number of worlds. Each world has at its center Mount Sumeru surrounded by seven oceans and seven rings of golden mountains separating them. Outside of this are four continents and eight subcontinents. Humans reside on the southern continent of Jambudvipa. One thousand of these worlds constitute a thousandfold world system. A thousand of these makes up a second-order thousandfold world system. Then, when multiplied a thousand times further, this makes a third-order world system or trichiliocosm, a universe of a billion worlds.

Tripitaka: The canon of Buddhist scriptures known as "Three Baskets." It is divided into three categories: the sutras (teachings of the Buddha), the vinaya (precepts and rules), and the abhidharma (commentaries on the Buddha's teachings).

Triple Gem: The Buddha, the Dharma, and Sangha. Referred to as "gems" to indicate their great value, also called the Triple Jewel, or the Three Jewels. The Buddha is the fully awakened or enlightened one; the Dharma is the teachings imparted by the Buddha; and the Sangha indicates the community of monastic members.

Western Pure Land of Ultimate Bliss: The realm where Amitabha Buddha presides. It came into existence due to Amitahba Buddha's forty-eight great vows. Sentient beings can make a vow to be reborn there, where they can practice without obstructions until they attain enlightenment.

World-honored One: One of the ten epithets of the Buddha.

Yama: Lord of death. He is said to supervise the hell realm.

About the Author

Venerable Master Hsing Yun is a Chinese Buddhist monk, author, philanthropist, and founder of the Fo Guang Shan monastic order, which has branches throughout Asia, Europe, Africa, Australia, and the Americas. Ordained at the age of twelve in Jiangsu Province, China, Hsing Yun has spent over seventy years as a Buddhist monk promoting what he calls "Humanistic Buddhism"—Buddhism that meets the needs of people and is integrated into all aspects of daily life.

In 1949, Hsing Yun went to Taiwan and began to nurture the burgeoning Buddhist culture on the island. Early on in his monastic career, he was involved in promoting Buddhism through the written word. He has served as an editor and contributor for many Buddhist magazines and periodicals, authoring the daily columns "Between Ignorance and Enlightenment," "Dharma Words," and "Hsing Yun's Chan Talk." In 1957, he started his own Buddhist magazine, *Awakening the World*, and in 2000, the first daily Buddhist newspaper, the *Merit Times*.

Hsing Yun has authored more than one hundred books on how to bring happiness, peace, compassion and wisdom into daily life. These works include the *Song of Silence*, the *Biography of Sakyamuni Buddha*, and *National Master Yulin*. He also edited and published the *Fo Guang Encyclopedia*, the most authoritative Buddhist reference work in the Chinese language. His contributions have reached as far as sponsoring Buddhist music and art to creating Buddhist programming for television, radio, and the stage.

Today Master Hsing Yun continues to travel around the world teaching the Dharma. In 2010 he delivered around 120 lectures and gave nearly 30 interviews for television and radio. He continues to write a daily column for the *Merit Times*, as well as to produce one-stroke calligraphy paintings. He is also the acting president of Buddha's Light International Association (BLIA), the worldwide lay Buddhist service organization.

About Buddha's Light Publishing

Buddha's Light Publishing offers quality translations of classical Buddhist texts as well as works by contemporary Buddhist teachers and scholars. We embrace Humanistic Buddhism, and promote Buddhist writing which is accessible, community-oriented, and relevant to daily life.

Founded in 1996 by Venerable Master Hsing Yun as the Fo Guang Shan International Translation Center, Buddha's Light Publishing seeks to continue Master Hsing Yun's goal of promoting the Buddha's teachings by fostering writing, art, and culture. Learn more by visiting www.blpusa.com.